The buddhist Catechism,
The Life of Buddha and its Lessons,
The Golden Rules of Buddhism,
(3 Books)

HENRY S. OLCOTT

2015 by McAllister Editions (MCALLISTEREDITIONS@GMAIL.COM). This book is a classic, and a product of its time. It does not reflect the same views on ___ gender, sexuality, ethnicity, and interpersonal relations as it would if it

CONTENTS

BOOK ONE

THE BUDDHIST CATECHISM

DEDICATION

In token of respect and affection I dedicate to my counsellor and friend of many years, Hikkaduwe Sumangala, Pradhāna Nāyaka Sthavīra and High Priest of Adam's Peak (Sripada) and the Western Province, THE BUDDHIST CATECHISM, in its revised form.

H. S. OLCOTT

Adyar, 1903.

CERTIFICATE TO THE FIRST EDITION

VIDYODAYA COLLEGE,

Colombo, 7th July, 1881.

I hereby certify that I have carefully examined the Sinhalese version of the Catechism prepared by Colonel H. S. Olcott, and that the same is in agreement with the Canon of the Southern Buddhist Church. I recommend the work to teachers in Buddhist schools, mid to all others who may wish to impart information to beginners about the essential features of our religion.

H. SUMANGALA,

High Priest of Sripada and Galle, and Principal of the Vidyodaya Parivena.

VIDYODAYA COLLEGE,

April 7, 1897.

I have gone over the thirty-third (English) edition of the Catechism, with the help of interpreters, and confirm my recommendation for its use in Buddhist schools.

H. SUMANGALA.

PREFACE

TO THE THIRTY-THIRD EDITION

In the working out of my original plan, I have added more questions and answers in the text of each new English edition of the Catechism, leaving it to its translators to render them into whichever of the other vernaculars they may be working in. The unpretending aim in view is to give so succinct and yet comprehensive a digest of Buddhistic history, ethics and philosophy as to enable beginners to understand and appreciate the noble ideal taught by the Buddha, and thus make it easier for them to follow out the Dharma in its details. In the present edition a great many new questions and answers have been introduced, while the matter has been grouped within five categories, *viz.*: (1) The Life of the Buddha; (2) the Doctrine; (3) the Sangha, or monastic order; (4) a brief history of Buddhism, its Councils and propaganda; (5) some reconciliation of Buddhism with science. This, it is believed, will largely increase the value of the little book, and make it even more suitable for use in Buddhist schools, of which, in Ceylon, over one hundred have already been opened by the Sinhalese people under the general supervision of the Theosophical Society. In preparing this edition I have received valuable help from some of my oldest and best qualified Sinhalese colleagues. The original edition was gone over with me word by word, by that eminent scholar and bhikkhu, H. Sumangala, Pradhāna Nāyaka, and the Assistant Principal of his Pālī College at Colombo, Hyeyantuduve Anunayaka Terunnanse; and the High Priest has also kindly scrutinised the present revision and given me invaluable points to embody. It has the merit, therefore, of being a fair presentation of the Buddhism of the "Southern Church," chiefly derived from first-hand sources. The Catechism has been published in twenty languages, mainly by Buddhists, for Buddhists.

H. S. O.

ADYAR, 17th *May*, 1897.

PREFACE

The popularity of this little work seems undiminished, edition after edition being called for. While the present one was in the press a second German edition, re-translated by the learned Dr. Erich Bischoff, was published at Leipzig, by the Griebens Co., and a third translation into French, by my old friend and colleague, Commandant D. A. Courmes, was being got ready at Paris. A fresh version in Sinhalese is also preparing at Colombo. It is very gratifying to a declared Buddhist like myself to read what so ripe a scholar as Mr. G. R. S. Mead, author of*Fragments of of a Faith Forgotten, Pistis Sophia,* and many other works on Christian origins, thinks of the value of the compilation. He writes in the *Theosophical Review*: "It has been translated into no less than twenty different languages, and may be said without the faintest risk of contradiction, to have been the busiest instrument of Buddhist propaganda for many a day in the annals of that long somnolent dharma. The least that learned Buddhists of Ceylon can do to repay the debt of gratitude they owe to Colonel Olcott and other members of the Theosophical Society who have worked for them, is to bestir themselves to throw some light on their own origins and doctrines."

I am afraid we shall have to wait long for this help to come from the Buddhist bhikkhus, almost the only learned men of Ceylon; at least I have not been able during an intimate intercourse of twenty-two years, to arouse their zeal. It has always seemed to me incongruous that an American, making no claims at all to scholarship, should be looked to by the Sinhalese to help them teach the dharma to their children; and as I believe I have said in an earlier edition, I only consented to write THE BUDDHIST CATECHISM after I had found that no bhikkhu would undertake it. Whatever its demerits, I can at least say that the work contains the essence of some 15,000 pages of Buddhist teaching that I have read in connexion with my work.

H. S. O.

ADYAR, *7th February,* 1903.

PREFACE

TO THE FORTIETH EDITION

The popularity of this little work is proved by the constant demand for new editions, in English and other languages. In looking over the matter for the present edition, I have found very little to change or to add, for the work seems to present a very fair idea of the contents of Southern Buddhism; and, as my object is never to write an extended essay on the subject, I resist the temptation to wander off into amplifications of details which, however interesting to the student of comparative religion, are useless in a rational scheme of elementary instruction.

The new Sinhalese version (38th edition) which is being prepared by my respected friend, D. B. Jayatilaka, Principal of Ānanda (Buddhist) College, Colombo, is partly printed, but cannot be completed until he is relieved of some of the pressure upon his time. The Tamil version (41st edition) has been undertaken by the leaders of the Pañchama community of Madras, and will shortly issue from the press. The Spanish version (39th edition) is in the hands of my friend, Señor Xifré, and the French one (37th edition) in those of Commandant Courmes.

So the work goes on, and by this unpretending agency the teachings of the Buddha Dharma are being carried throughout the world.

H. S. O.

ADYAR, 7th January, 1905.

PREFACE

TO THE FORTY-SECOND EDITION

The writer of this Catechism has passed away from earth, but, before he left the body, he had arranged with the High Priest Sumangala to make some small corrections in the text. These are incorporated in the present edition by the High Priest's wish, expressed to me in Colombo, in November 1907.

I have not altered the numbering of the questions, as it might cause confusion in a class to change the numbers, if some pupils had the older editions and some the new.

ADYAR,　　　)

17th February, 1908.)　　　ANNIE BESANT

PART I. THE LIFE OF THE BUDDHA

1. Question. *Of what religion* are you?*

Answer. The Buddhist.

* The word "religion" is most inappropriate to apply to Buddhism which is not a religion, but a moral philosophy, as I have shown later on. But, by common usage the word has been applied to all groups of people who profess a special moral doctrine, and is so employed by statisticians. The Sinhalese Buddhists have never yet had any conception of what Europeans imply in the etymological construction of the Latin root of this term. In their creed there is no such thing as a "binding" in the Christian sense—a submission to or merging of self in a Divine Being. *Āgama* is their vernacular word to express their relation to Buddhism and the BUDDHA. It is pure Samskrt, and means "approach, or coming"; and as "*Buddha*" is enlightenment, the compound word by which they indicate Buddhism—*Buddhāgama*—would be properly rendered as "an approach or coming to enlightenment," or possibly as a following of the Doctrine of SĀKYAMUNI. The missionaries, finding *Āgama* ready to their hand, adopted it as the equivalent for "religion"; and Christianity is written by them*Christianāgama*, whereas it should be *Christianibandhana*, for *bandhana* is the etymological equivalent for "religion". The name *Vibhajja vāda*—one who analyses—is another name given to a Buddhist, and Advayavādī is a third. With this explanation, I continue to employ under protest the familiar word when speaking of Buddhistic philosophy, for the convenience of the ordinary reader.

2. Q. *What is Buddhism?*

A. It is a body of teachings given out by the great personage known as the Buddha.

3. Q. *Is "Buddhism" the best name for this teaching?*

A. No; that is only a western term: the best name for it is Bauddha Dharma.

4. Q. *Would you call a person a Buddhist who had merely been born of Buddha parents?*

A. Certainly not. A Buddhist is one who not only professes belief in the Buddha as the noblest of Teachers, in the Doctrine preached by Him, and in the Brotherhood of Arhats, but practises His precepts in daily life.

5. Q. *What is a male lay Buddhist called?*

A. An Upāsaka.

6. Q. *What a female?*

A. An Upāsika.

7. Q. *When was this doctrine first preached?*

A. There is some disagreement as to the actual date, but according to the Sinhalese Scriptures it was in the year 2513 of the (present) Kali-Yuga.

8. Q. *Give the important dates in the last birth of the Founder?*

A. He was born under the constellation Visā on a Tuesday in May, in the year 2478 (K.Y.); he retired to the jungle in the year 2506; became Buddha in 2513; and, passing out of the round of rebirths, entered Paranirvāna in the year 2558, aged eighty years. Each of these events happened on a day of full moon, so all are conjointly celebrated in the great festival of the full-moon of the month Wesak (*Vaisākha*), corresponding to the month of May.

9. Q. *Was the Buddha God?*

A. No. Buddha Dharma teaches no "divine" incarnation.

10. Q. *Was he a man?*

A. Yes; but the wisest, noblest and most holy being, who had developed himself in the course of countless births far beyond all other beings, the previous BUDDHAS alone excepted.

11. Q. *Were there other Buddhas before him?*

A. Yes; as will be explained later on.

12. Q. *Was Buddha his name?*

A. No. It is the name of a condition or state of mind, of the mind after it has reached the culmination of development.

13. Q. *What is its meaning?*

A. Enlightened; or, he who has the all-perfect wisdom. The Pālī phrase is *Sabbannu*, the One of Boundless Knowledge. In Samskrt it is *Sarvajña*.

14. Q. *What was the Buddha's real name then?*

A. SIDDHĀRTHA was his royal name, and GAUTAMA, or GOTAMA, his family name. He was Prince of Kapilavāstu and belonged to the illustrious family of the Okkāka, of the Solar race.

15. Q. *Who were his father and mother?*

A. King Suddhodana and Queen Māyā, called Mahā Māyā.

16. Q. *What people did this King reign over?*

A. The Sākyas; an Aryan tribe of Kshattriyas.

17. Q. *Where was Kapilavāstu?*

A. In India, one hundred miles north-east of the City of Benares, and about forty miles from the Himalaya mountains. It is situated in the Nepāl Terai. The city is now in ruins.

18. Q. *On what river?*

A. The Rohīnī, now called the Kohana.

19. Q. *Tell me again when Prince Siddhārtha was born?*

A. Six hundred and twenty-three years before the Christian era.

20. Q. *Is the exact spot known?*

A. It is now identified beyond question. An archaeologist in the service of the Government of India has discovered in the jungle of the Nepāl Terai a stone pillar erected by the mighty Buddhist sovereign, Asoka, to mark the very spot. The place was known in those times as the Lumbinī Garden.

21. Q. *Had the Prince luxuries and splendours like other Princes?*

A. He had; his father, the King, built him three magnificent palaces— for the three Indian seasons—the cold, the hot, and the rainy—of nine, five, and three stories respectively, and handsomely decorated.

22. Q. *How were they situated?*

A. Around each palace were gardens of the most beautiful and fragrant flowers, with fountains of spouting water, the trees full of singing birds, and peacocks strutting over the ground.

23. Q. *Was he living alone?*

A. No; in his sixteenth year he was married to the Princess Yasodharā, daughter of the King Suprabuddha. Many beautiful maidens, skilled in dancing and music, were also in continual attendance to amuse him.

24. Q. *How did he get his wife?*

A. In the ancient Kshattriya or warrior fashion, by overcoming all competitors in games and exercises of skill and prowess, and then selecting Yasodharā out of all the young princesses, whose fathers had brought them to the tournament or *mela.*

25. Q. *How, amid all this luxury, could a Prince become all-wise?*

A. He had such natural wisdom that when but a child he seemed to understand all arts and sciences almost without study. He had the best teachers, but they could teach him nothing that he did not seem to comprehend immediately.

26. Q. *Did he become Buddha in his splendid palaces?*

A. No. He left all and went alone into the jungle.

27. Q. *Why did he do this?*

A. To discover the cause of our sufferings and the way to escape from them.

28. Q. *Was it not selfishness that made him do this?*

A. No; it was boundless love for all beings that made him devote himself to their good.

29. Q. *But how did he acquire this boundless love?*

A. Throughout numberless births and aeons of years he had been cultivating this love, with the unfaltering determination to become a Buddha.

30. Q. *What did he this time relinquish?*

A. His beautiful palaces, his riches, luxuries and pleasures, his soft beds, fine dresses, rich food, and his kingdom; he even left his beloved wife and only son, Rāhula.

31. Q. *Did any other man ever sacrifice so much for our sake?*

A. Not one in this present world-period: this is why Buddhists so love him, and why good Buddhists try to be like him.

32. Q. *But have not many men given up all earthly blessings, and even life itself, for the sake of their fellow-men?*

A. Certainly. But we believe that this surpassing unselfishness and love for humanity showed themselves in his renouncing the bliss of Nirvāna countless ages ago, when he was born as the Brāhmana Sumedha, in the time of Dīpānkara Buddha: he had then reached the stage where he might have entered Nirvāna, had he not loved mankind more than himself. This renunciation implied his voluntarily enduring the miseries of earthly lives until he became Buddha, for the sake of teaching all beings the way to emancipation and to give rest to the world.

33. Q. *How old was he when he went to the jungle?*

A. He was in his twenty-ninth year.

34. Q. *What finally determined him to leave all that men usually love so much and go to the jungle?*

A. A *Deva*[see defin.below] appeared to him when driving out in his chariot, under four impressive forms, on four different occasions.

35. Q. *What were these different forms?*

A. Those of a very old man broken down by age, of a sick man, of a decaying corpse, and of a dignified hermit.

36. Q. *Did he alone see these?*

A. No, his attendant, Channa, also saw them.

37. Q. *Why should these sights, so familiar to everybody, have caused him to go to the jungle?*

A. We often see such sights: he had not seen them, so they made a deep impression on his mind.

38. Q. *Why had he not also seen them?*

A. The Brāhmana astrologers had foretold at his birth that he would one day resign his kingdom and, become a BUDDHA. The King, his father, not wishing to lose an heir to his kingdom, had carefully prevented his seeing any sights that might suggest to him human misery and death. No one was allowed even to speak of such things to the Prince. He was almost like a prisoner in his lovely palaces and flower gardens. They were surrounded by high walls, and inside everything was made as beautiful as possible, so that he might not wish to go and see the sorrow and distress that are in the world.

39. Q. *Was he so kind-hearted that the King feared he might really wish to leave everything for the world's sake?*

A. Yes; he seems to have felt for all beings so strong a pity and love as that.

40. Q. *And how did he expect to learn the cause of sorrow in the jungle?*

A. By removing far away from all that could prevent his thinking deeply of the causes of sorrow and the nature of man.

41. Q. *How did he escape from the palace?*

A. One night, when all were asleep, he arose, took a last look at his sleeping wife and infant son; called Channa, mounted his favourite white horse Kanthaka, and rode to the palace gate. The *Devas* had thrown a deep sleep upon the King's guard who watched the gate, so that they could not hear the noise of the horse's hoofs.

42. Q. *But the gate was locked, was it not?*

A. Yes; but the *Devas* caused it to open without the slightest noise, and he rode away into the darkness.

43. Q. *Whither did he go?*

A. To the river Anomā, a long way from Kapilavāstu.

44. Q. *What did he then do?*

A. He sprang from his horse, cut off his beautiful hair with his sword, put on the yellow dress of an ascetic, and giving his ornaments and horse to Channa, ordered him to take them back to his father, the King.

45. Q. *What then?*

A. He went afoot towards Rājagrha, the capital city of King Bimbisāra, of Magadha.

46. Q. *Who visited him there?*

A. The King with his whole Court.[For an admirable account of this interview consult Dr. Paul Carus' *Gospel of Buddha*, page 20, *et seq.*]

46a. Q. *Thence whither did he go?*

A. To Uruvela, near the present Mahābōdhi Temple at Buddha Gayā.

47. Q. *Why did he go there?*

A. In the forests were hermits—very wise men, whose pupil he afterwards became, in the hope of finding the knowledge of which he was in search.

48. Q. *Of what religion were they?*

A. The Hindu religion: they were Brāhmanas.[*]

> *The term Hindū, once a contemptuous term, used by the Musalmāns to designate the people of Sindh, whom they conquered, is now used in an ecclesiastical sense.

49. Q. *What did they teach?*

A. That by severe penances and torture of the body a man may acquire perfect wisdom.

50. Q. *Did the Prince find this to be so?*

A. No; he learned their systems and practised all their penances, but he could not thus discover the cause of human sorrow and the way to absolute emancipation.

51. Q. *What did he then do?*

A. He went away into the forest near Uruvela, and spent six years in deep meditation, undergoing the severest discipline in mortifying his body.

52. Q. *Was he alone?*

A. No; five Brāhman companions attended him.

53. Q. *What were their names?*

A. Kondañña, Bhaddiya, Vappa, Mahānāma, and Assaji.

54. Q. *What plan of discipline did he adopt to open his mind to know the whole truth?*

A. He sat and meditated, concentrating his mind upon the higher problems of life, and shutting out from his sight and hearing all that was likely to interrupt his inward reflections.

55. Q. *Did he fast?*

A. Yes, through the whole period. He took less and less food and water until, it is said, he ate scarcely more than one grain of rice or of sesamum seed each day.

56. Q. *Did this give him the wisdom he longed for?*

A. No. He grew thinner and thinner in body and fainter in strength until, one day, as he was slowly walking about and meditating, his vital force suddenly left him and he fell to the ground unconscious.

57. Q. *What did his companions think of that?*

A. They fancied he was dead; but after a time he revived.

58. Q. *What then?*

A. The thought came to him that knowledge could never be reached by mere fasting or bodily suffering, but must be gained by the opening of the mind. He had just barely escaped death from self-starvation, yet had not obtained the Perfect Wisdom. So he decided to eat, that he might live at least long enough to become wise.

59. Q. *Who gave him food?*

A. He received food from Sujatā, a nobleman's daughter, who saw him sitting at the foot of a nyagrodha (banyan) tree. He arose, took his alms-bowl, bathed in the river Nerañjāra, ate the food, and went into the jungle.

60. Q. *What did he do there?*

A. Having formed his determination after these reflections, he went at evening to the Bōdhi, or Asvattha tree, where the present Mahābōdhi Temple stands.

61. Q. *What did he do there?*

A. He determined not to leave the spot until he attained perfect wisdom.

62. Q. *At which side of the tree did he seat himself?*

A. The side facing the east.[*]

*No reason is given in the canonical books for the choice of this side of the tree, though an explanation is to be found in the popular legends upon which the books of Bishop

Bigandet and other European commentators are based. There are always certain influences coming upon us from the different quarters of the sky. Sometimes the influence from one quarter will be best, sometimes that from another quarter. But the Buddha thought that the perfected man is superior to all extraneous influences.

63. Q. *What did he obtain that night?*

A. The knowledge of his previous births, of the causes of rebirths, and of the way to extinguish desires. Just before the break of the next day his mind was entirely opened, like the full-blown lotus flower; the light of supreme knowledge, or the Four Truths, poured in upon him. He had become BUDDHA—the Enlightened, the all-knowing—the Sarvajña.

64. Q. *Had he at last discovered the cause of human misery?*

A. At last he had. As the light of the morning sun chases away the darkness of night, and reveals to sight the trees, fields, rocks, seas, rivers, animals, men and all things, so the full light of knowledge rose in his mind, and he saw at one glance the causes of human suffering and the way to escape from them.

65. Q. *Had he great struggles before gaining this perfect wisdom?*

A. Yes, mighty and terrible struggles. He had to conquer in his body all those natural defects and human appetites and desires that prevent our seeing the truth. He had to overcome all the bad influences of the sinful world around him. Like a soldier fighting desperately in battle against many enemies, he struggled: like a hero who conquers, he gained his object, and the secret of human misery was discovered.

66. Q. *What use did he make of the knowledge thus gained?*

A. At first he was reluctant to teach it to the people at large.

67. Q. *Why?*

A. Because of its profound importance and sublimity. He feared that but few people would understand it.

68. Q. *What made him alter this view?*[*]

*The ancient story is that the God Brahmā himself implored him not to withhold the glorious truth.

A. He saw that it was his duty to teach what he had learnt as clearly and simply as possible, and trust to the truth impressing itself upon the popular mind in proportion to each one's individual Karma. It was the only way of salvation, and every being had an equal right to have it pointed out to him. So he determined to begin with his five late companions, who had abandoned him when he broke his fast.

69. Q. *Where did he find them?*

A. In the deer-park at Isipatana, near Benares.

70. Q. *Can the spot be now identified?*

A. Yes, a partly ruined stūpa, or dagoba, is still standing on that very spot.

71. Q. *Did those five companions readily listen to him?*

A. At first, no; but so great was the spiritual beauty of his appearance, so sweet and convincing his teaching, that they soon turned and gave him the closest attention.

72. Q. *What effect did this discourse have upon them?*

A. The aged Kondañña, one who "understood" (*Anna*), was the first to lose his prejudices, accept the Buddha's teaching, become his disciple, and enter the Path leading to Arhatship. The other four soon followed his example.

73. Q. *Who were his next converts?*

A. A rich young layman, named Yasa, and his father, a wealthy merchant. By the end of three months the disciples numbered sixty persons.

74. Q. *Who were the first women lay disciples?*

A. The mother and wife of Yasa.

75. Q. *What did the Buddha do at that time?*[*]

A. He called the disciples together, gave them full instructions, and sent them out in all directions to preach his doctrine.

*Brāhmanism not being offered to non-Hindūs, Buddhism is consequently, the oldest missionary religion in the world. The early missionaries endured every hardship, cruelty, and persecution, with unfaltering courage.

76. Q. *What was the essence of it?*

A. That the way of emancipation lies in leading the holy life and following the rules laid down, which will be explained later on.

77. Q. *Tell me what name he gave to this course of life?*

A. The Noble Eightfold Path.

78. Q. *How is it called in the Pālī language?*

A. *Ariyo atthangiko maggo.*

79. Q. *Whither did the Buddha then go?*

A. To Uruvela.

80. Q. *What happened there?*

A. He converted a man named Kāshyapa, renowned for his learning and teacher of the Jatilas, a great sect of fire-worshippers, all of whom became also his followers.

81. Q. *Who was his next great convert?*

A. King Bimbisāra, of Magadha.

82. Q. *Which two of the Buddha's most learned and beloved disciples were converted at about this time?*

A. Sāriputra and Moggallāna, formerly chief disciples of Sañjaya, the ascetic.

83. Q. *For what did they become renowned?*

A. Sāriputra for his profound learning (*Prajña*), Moggallāna for his exceptional spiritual powers (*Iddhi*).

84. Q. *Are these wonder-working powers miraculous?*

A. No, but natural to all men and capable of being developed by a certain course of training.

85. Q. *Did the Buddha hear again from his family after leaving them?*

A. Oh yes, seven years later, while he was living at Rājagrha, his father. King Suddhodana, sent a message to request him to come and let him see him again before he died.

86. Q. *Did he go?*

A. Yes. His father went with all his relatives and ministers to meet him and received him with great joy.

87. Q. *Did he consent to resume his old rank?*

A. No. In all sweetness he explained to his father that the Prince Siddhārtha had passed out of existence, as such, and was now changed into the condition of a Buddha, to whom all beings were equally akin and equally dear. Instead of ruling over one tribe or nation, like an earthly king, he, through his Dharma, would win the hearts of all men to be his followers.

88. Q. *Did he see Yasodharā and his son Rāhula?*

A. Yes. His wife, who had mourned for him with deepest love, wept bitterly. She also sent Rāhula to ask him to give him his inheritance, as the son of a prince.

89. Q. *What happened?*

A. To one and all he preached the Dharma as the cure for all sorrows. His father, son, wife, Ānanda (his half-brother), Devadatta (his cousin and brother-in-law), were all converted and became his disciples. Two other famous ones were Anuruddha, afterwards a great metaphysician, and Upāli, a barber, afterwards the greatest authority on Vinaya. Both of these gained great renown.

90. Q. *Who was the first Bhikkuni?*

A. Prajāpatī, the aunt and foster-mother of Prince Siddhārtha. With her, Yasodharā and many other ladies were admitted into the Order as *Bhikkhunis* or female devotees.

91. Q. *What effect did the taking up of the religious life by his sons, Siddhārtha and Ānanda, his nephew, Devadatta, his son's wife, Yasudharā, and his grandson, Rāhula, have upon the old King Suddhodana?*

A. It grieved him much and he complained to the Buddha, who then made it a rule of the Order that no person should thenceforth be ordained without the consent of his parents if alive.

92. Q. *Tell me about the fate of Devadatta?*

A. He was a man of great intelligence and rapidly advanced in the knowledge of the Dharma, but being also extremely ambitious, he came to envy and hate the Buddha, and at last plotted to kill him. He also influenced Ajātashatru, son of King Bimbisāra, to murder his noble father, and to become his—Devadatta's—disciple.

93. Q. *Did he do any injury to the Buddha?*

A. Not the least, but the evil he plotted against him recoiled upon himself, and he met with an awful death.

94. Q. *For how many years was the Buddha engaged in teaching?*

A. Forty-five years, during which time he preached a great many discourses. His custom and that of his disciples was to travel and preach during the eight dry months, but during the season of Way—the rains—he and they would stop in the pānsulas and vihāras which had been built for them by various kings and other wealthy converts.

95. Q. *Which were the most famous of these buildings?*

A. Jetāvanārāma; Veluvanārāma; Pubbārāma; Nigrodhārāma and Isipatanārāma.

96. Q. *What kind of people were converted by him and his disciples?*

A. People of all ranks, nations and castes; rājas and coolies, rich and poor, mighty and humble, the illiterate and the most learned. His doctrine was suited to all.

97. Q. *Give some account of the decease of the Buddha?*

A. In the forty-fifth season after his attaining Buddhahood, on the full-moon day of May, knowing that his end was near, he came at evening to Kusināgāra, a place about one hundred and twenty miles from Benares. In the sāla grove of the Mallas, the Uparvartana of Kusināgāra, between two sāla trees, he had his bedding spread with the head towards the north according to the ancient custom. He lay upon it, and with his mind perfectly clear, gave his final instructions to his disciples and bade them farewell.

98. Q. *Did he also make new converts in those last tours?*

A. Yes, a very important one, a great Brāhmana pandit named Subhadra. He had also preached to the Mallya princes and their followers.

99. Q. *At day-break what happened?*

A. He passed into the interior condition of *Samādhi* and thence into Nirvāna.

100. Q. *What were his last words to his disciples?*

A. "Bhikkhus," he said, "I now impress it upon you, the parts and powers of man must be dissolved. Work out your salvation with diligence."

101. Q. *What convincing proof have we that the Buddha, formerly Prince Siddhārtha, was a historical personage?*

A. His existence is apparently as clearly proved as that of any other character of ancient history.

102. Q. *Name some of the proofs?*

A. (1) The testimony of those who personally knew him.

(2) The discovery of places and the remains of buildings mentioned in the narrative of his time.

(3) The rock-inscriptions, pillars and dagobas made in memory of him by sovereigns who were near enough to his time to be able to verify the story of his life.

(4) The unbroken existence of the Sangha which he founded, and their possession of the facts of his life transmitted from generation to generation from the beginning.

(5) The fact that in the very year of his death and at various times subsequently, conventions and councils of the Sangha were held, for the verification of the actual teachings of the Founder, and the handing down of those verified teachings from teacher to pupil, to the present day.

(6) After his cremation his relics were divided among eight kings and a stūpa was erected over each portion. The portion given to King Ajātashatru, and by him covered with a stūpa at Rājagrha, was taken, less than two centuries later, by the Emperor Asoka and distributed throughout his Empire. He, of course, had ample means of knowing whether the relics were those of the Buddha or not, since they had been in charge of the royal house of Patna from the beginning.

(7) Many of the Buddha's disciples, being Arhats and thus having control over their vital powers, must have lived to great ages, and there was nothing to have prevented two or three of them, in succession to each other, to have covered the whole period between the death of the Buddha and the reign of Asoka, and thus to have enabled the latter to get from his contemporary every desired attestation of the fact of the Buddha's life.* (*At the Second Council there were two pupils of Ānanda, consequently centenarians, while in Asoka's Council there were pupils of those pupils.)

(8) The "Mahāvansa," the best authenticated ancient history known to us, records the events of Sinhalese history to the reign of King Vijaya, 543 B.C.—almost the time of the Buddha—and gives most particulars of his life, as well as those of the Emperor Asoka and all other sovereigns related to Buddhistic history.

103. Q. *By what names of respect is the Buddha called?*

A. Sākyamuni (the Sākya Sage); Sākya-Simha (the Sākyan Lion); Sugata (the Happy One); Satthta (the Teacher); Jina (the Conqueror), Bhagavat (the Blessed One); Lokanātha (the Lord of the World); Sarvajña (the Omniscient One); Dharmarāja (the King of Truth); Tathāgata (the Great Being), etc.

PART II. THE DHARMA OR DOCTRINE

106. Q. *What is the meaning of the word Buddha?*

A. The enlightened, or he who has the perfect wisdom.

107. Q. *You have said that there were other Buddhas before this one?*

A. Yes; our belief is that, under the operation of eternal causation, a Buddha takes birth at intervals, when mankind have become plunged into misery through ignorance, and need the wisdom which it is the function of a Buddha to teach. (See also Q. 11.)

108. Q. *How is a Buddha developed?*

A. A person, hearing and seeing one of the Buddhas on earth, becomes seized with the determination so to live that at some future time, when he shall become fitted for it, he also will be a Buddha for the guiding of mankind out of the cycle of rebirth.

109. Q. *How does he proceed?*

A. Throughout that birth and every succeeding one, he strives to subdue his passions, to gain wisdom by experience, and to develop his higher faculties. He thus grows by degrees wiser, nobler in character, and stronger in virtue, until, finally, after numberless re-births he reaches the state when he can become Perfected, Enlightened, All-wise, the ideal Teacher of the human race.

110. Q. *While this gradual development is going on throughout all these births, by what name do we call him?*

A. Bōdhisat, or Bōdhisattva. Thus the Prince Siddhartha Gautama was a Bōdhisattva up to the moment when, under the blessed Bōdhi tree at Gayā, he became Buddha.

111. Q. *Have we any account of his various rebirths as a Bodhisattva?*

A. In the Jātakatthakathā, a book containing stories of the Bōdhisattva's reincarnations, there are several hundred tales of that kind.

112. Q. *What lesson do these stories teach?*

A. That a man can carry, throughout a long series of reincarnations, one great, good purpose which enables him to conquer bad tendencies and develop virtuous ones.

113. Q. *Can we fix the number of reincarnations through which a Bōdhisattva must pass before he can become a Buddha?*

A. Of course not: that depends upon his natural character, the state of development to which he has arrived when he forms the resolution to become a Buddha, and other things.

114. Q. *Have we a way of classifying Bōdhisattvas? If so, explain it.*

A. Bōdhisattvas—the future Buddhas—are divided into three classes.

115. Q. *Proceed. How are these three kinds of Bōdhisats named?*

A. Pannādhika, or Udghatitajña—"he who attains least quickly"; Saddhādhika, or Vipachitajña—"he who attains less quickly"; and Viryādhika, or Gneyya—"he who attains quickly". The Pannādhika Bōdhisats take the course of Intelligence; the Saddhādhika take the course of Faith; the Viryaāhika take the course of energetic Action. The first is guided by Intelligence and does not hasten; the second is full of Faith, and does not care to take the guidance of Wisdom; and the third never delays to do what is good. Regardless of the consequences to himself, he does it when he sees that it is best that it should be done.

116. Q. *When our Bōdhisattva became Buddha, what did he see was the cause of human misery? Tell me in one word.*

A. Ignorance (Avidyā).

117. Q. *Can you tell me the remedy?*

A. To dispel Ignorance and become wise (Prājña).

118. Q. *Why does ignorance cause suffering?*

A. Because it makes us prize what is not worth prizing, grieve when we should not grieve, consider real what is not real but only illusionary, and pass our lives in the pursuit of worthless objects, neglecting what is in reality most valuable.

119. Q. *And what is that which is most valuable?*

A. To know the whole secret of man's existence and destiny, so that we may estimate at no more than their actual value this life and its relations; and so that we may live in a way to ensure the greatest happiness and the least suffering for our fellow-men and ourselves.

120. Q. *What is the light that can dispel this ignorance of ours and remove all sorrows?*

A. The knowledge of the "Four Noble Truths," as the Buddha called them.

121. Q. *Name these Four Noble Truths?*

A. 1. The miseries of evolutionary existence resulting in births and deaths, life after life.

2. The cause productive of misery, which is the selfish desire, ever renewed, of satisfying one's self, without being able ever to secure that end.

3. The destruction of that desire, or the estranging of one's self from it.

4. The means of obtaining this destruction of desire.

122. Q. *Tell me some things that cause sorrow?*

A. Birth, decay, illness, death, separation from objects we love, association with those who are repugnant, craving for what cannot be obtained.

123. Q. *Do these differ with each individual?*

A. Yes: but all men suffer from them in degree.

124. Q. *How can we escape the sufferings which result from unsatisfied desires and ignorant cravings?*

A. By complete conquest over, and destruction of, this eager thirst for life and its pleasures, which causes sorrow.

125. Q. *How may we gain such a conquest?*

A. By following the Noble Eight-fold Path which the Buddha discovered and pointed out.

126. Q. *What do you mean by that word: what is this Noble Eight-fold Path?* (For the Pālī name see Q.79 supra.)

A. The eight parts of this path are called *angas*. They are: 1. Right Belief (as to the law of Causation, or Karma); 2. Right Thought; 3. Right Speech; 4. Right Action; 5. Right Means of Livelihood; 6. Right Exertion; 7. Right Remembrance and Self-discipline; 8. Right Concentration of Thought. The man who keeps these *angas* in mind and follows them will be free from sorrow and ultimately reach salvation.

127. Q. *Can you give a better word for salvation?*

A. Yes, emancipation.

128. Q. *Emancipation, then, from what?*

A. Emancipation from the miseries of earthly existence and of rebirths, all of which are due to ignorance and impure lusts and cravings.

129. Q. *And when this salvation or emancipation is attained, what do we reach?*

A. NIRVĀNA.

130. Q. *What is Nirvāna?*

A. A condition of total cessation of changes, of perfect rest, of the absence of desire and illusion and sorrow, of the total obliteration of everything that goes to make up the physical man. Before reaching Nirvāna man is constantly being reborn; when he reaches Nirvāna he is born no more.

131. Q. *Where can be found a learned discussion of the word Nirvāna and a list of the other names by which the old Pālī writers attempt to define it?*

A. In the famous Dictionary of the Pālī Language, by the late Mr. B. O. Childers, is a complete list.[*]

*Mr. Childers takes a highly pessimistic view of the Nirvānic state, regarding it as annihilation. Later students disagree with him.

132. Q. *But some people imagine that Nirvāna is some sort of heavenly place, a Paradise. Does Buddhism teach that?*

A. No. When Kūtadanta asked the Buddha "Where is Nirvāna," he replied that it was "wherever the precepts are obeyed".

133. Q. *What causes us to be reborn?*

A. The unsatisfied selfish desire (Skt., *trshnā*; Pālī, tanhā) for things that belong to the state of personal existence in the material world. This unquenched thirst for physical existence (*bhāva*) is a force, and has a creative power in itself so strong that it draws the being back into mundane life.

134. Q. *Are our rebirths in any way affected by the nature of our unsatisfied desires?*

A. Yes, and by our individual merits or demerits.

135. Q. *Does our merit or demerit control the state, condition or form in which we shall be re-born?*

A. It does. The broad rule is that if we have an excess of merit we shall be well and happily born the next time; if an excess of demerit, our next birth will be wretched and full of suffering.

136. Q. *One chief pillar of Buddhistic doctrine is, then, the idea that every effect is the result of an actual cause, is it not?*

. It is; of a cause either immediate or remote.

137. Q. *What do we call this causation?*

A. Applied to individuals, it is Karma, that is, action. It means that our own actions or deeds bring upon us whatever of joy or misery we experience.

138. Q. *Can a bad man escape from the outworkings of his Karma?*

A. The *Dhammapada* says: "There exists no spot on the earth, or in the sky, or in the sea, neither is there any in the mountain-clefts, where an (evil) deed does not bring trouble (to the doer)."

139. Q. *Can a good man escape?*

A. As the result of deeds of peculiar merit, a man may attain certain advantages of place, body, environment and teaching in his next stage of progress, which ward off the effects of bad Karma and help his higher evolution.

140. *What are they called?*

A. *Gati Sampatti, Upādhi Sampatti, Kāla Sampatti* and *Payoga Sampatti.*

141. Q. *Is that consistent or inconsistent with common sense and the teachings of modern science?*

A. Perfectly consistent: there can be no doubt of it.

142. Q. *May all men become Buddhas?*

A. It is not in the nature of every man to become a Buddha; for a Buddha is developed only at long intervals of time, and seemingly, when the state of humanity absolutely requires such a teacher to show it the forgotten Path to Nirvāna. But every being may equally reach Nirvāna, by conquering Ignorance and gaining Wisdom.

143. Q. *Does Buddhism teach that man is reborn only upon our earth?*

A. As a general rule that would be the case, until he had evolved beyond its level; but the inhabited worlds are numberless. The world upon which a person is to have his next birth, as well as the nature of the rebirth itself, is decided by the preponderance of the individual's merit or demerit. In other words, it will be controlled by his attractions, as science would describe it; or by his Karma, as we, Buddhists, would say.

144. Q. *Are there worlds more perfectly developed, and others less so than our Earth?*

A. Buddhism teaches that there are whole *Sakwalas*, or systems of worlds, of various kinds, higher and lower, and also that the inhabitants of each world correspond in development with itself.

145. Q. *Has not the Buddha summed up his whole doctrine in one gāthā, or verse?*

A. Yes.

146. Q. *Repeat it?*

A. *Sabba pāpassa akaranm,*
Kusalassa upasampadā
Sachitta pariyo dapanam—
Etam Buddhānusāsanam.

"To cease from all evil actions,

To generate all that is good,

To cleanse one's mind:

This is the constant advice of the Buddhas."

147. Q. *Have the first three of these lines any very striking characteristics?*

A. Yes: the first line embodies the whole spirit of the *Vinaya Pitaka*, the second that of the *Sutta*, the third that of the *Abhidhamma*. They comprise only eight Pālī words, yet, as the dew-drop reflects the stars, they sparkle with the spirit of all the Buddha Dharma.

148. Q. *Do these precepts show that Buddhism is an active or a passive religion?*

A. To "cease from sin" may be called passive, but to "get virtue" and "to cleanse one's own heart," or mind, are altogether *active* qualities. Buddha taught that we should not merely not be evil, but that we should be*positively* good.

149. Q. *Who or what are the "Three Guides"[*] that a Buddhist Is supposed to follow?*

A. They are disclosed in the formula called the Tisarana: "I follow Buddha as my Guide: I follow the Law as my Guide: I follow the Order as my Guide." These three *are*, in fact, the Buddha Dharma.

* *Saranam*. Wijesinha Mudaliar writes me: "This word has been hitherto very inappropriately and erroneously rendered *Refuge*, by European Pālī scholars, and thoughtlessly so accepted by native Pālī scholars. Neither Pālī etymology nor Buddhistic philosophy justifies the translation. *Refuge*, in the sense of a *fleeing back or a place of shelter*, is quite foreign to true Buddhism, which insists on every man working out his own emancipation. The root *Sr* in Samskrt (*sara* in Pālī) means to move, to go; so that *Suranim* would denote a moving, or he or that which goes before or with another—a Guide or Helper. I construe the passage thus: *Gachchāmi*, I go, *Buddham*, to Buddha *Saranam*, as my Guide. The translation of the*Tisarana* as the "Three Refuges," has given rise to much misapprehension, and has been made by anti-Buddhists a fertile pretext for taunting Buddhists with the absurdity of taking refuge in non-entities and believing in unrealities. The term refuge is more applicable to Nirvāna, of which *Saranam* is a synonym. The High Priest Sumangala also calls my attention to the fact that the Pālī root *Sara* has the secondary meaning of killing, or that which destroys. *Buddham saranam gachchāmi* might thus be rendered "I go to Buddha, the Law, and the Order, as the destroyers of my fears—the first by his preaching, the second by its axiomatic truth, the third by their various examples and precepts."

150. Q. *What does he mean when repeating this formula?*

A. He means that he regards the Buddha as his all-wise Teacher, Friend and Exemplar; the Law, or Doctrine, as containing the essential and immutable principles of Justice and Truth and the path that leads to the realisation of perfect peace of mind on earth; and the Order as the teachers and exemplars of that excellent Law taught by Buddha.

151. Q. *But are not some of the members of this "Order" men intellectually and morally inferior?*

A. Yes; but we are taught by the Buddha that only those who diligently attend to the Precepts, discipline their minds, and strive to attain or have attained one of the eight stages of holiness and perfection, constitute his "Order". It is expressly stated that the Order referred to in the "Tisarana" refers to the "Attha Ariya Puggala"—the Noble Ones who have attained one of the eight stages of perfection. The mere wearing of yellow robes, or even ordination, does not of itself make a man pure or wise or entitle him to reverence.

152. Q. *Then it is not such unworthy bhikkhus as they, whom the true Buddhist would lake as his guides?*

A. Certainly not.

153. Q. *What are the five observances, or universal precepts, called the Pañcha Sīla, which are imposed on the laity in general?*

A. They are included in the following formula,, which Buddhists repeat publicly at the vihāras (temples):

I observe the precept to refrain from destroying the life of beings.

I observe the precept to refrain from stealing.

I observe the precept to abstain from unlawful sexual intercourse.[*]

*This qualified form refers, of course, to laymen who only profess to keep five precepts; a Bhikkhu must observe strict celibacy. So, also, must the laic who binds himself to observe eight of the whole ten Precepts for specified periods; during these periods he must be celibate. The five Precepts were laid down by Buddha for all people. Though one may not be a Buddhist, yet the five and eight Precepts may profitably bo observed by all. It is the taking of the "Three

Refuges" that constitutes one a Buddhist.

I observe the precept to refrain from falsehood.

I observe the precept to abstain from using intoxicants.

154. Q. What strikes the intelligent person on reading these Sīlas?

A. That one who observes them strictly must escape from every cause productive of human misery. If we study history we shall find that it has all sprung from one or another of these causes.

155. Q. In which Sīlas is the far-seeing wisdom of the Buddha most plainly shown?

A. In the first, third and fifth; for the taking of life, sensuality, and the use of intoxicants, cause at least ninety-five per cent of the sufferings among men.

156. Q. *What benefits does a man derive from the observance of these Precepts?*

A. He is said to acquire more or less merit according to the manner and time of observing the precepts, and the number observed; that is, if he observes only one precept, violating the other four, he acquires the merit of the observance of that precept only; and the longer he keeps that precept the greater will be the merit. He who keeps all the precepts inviolate will cause himself to have a higher and happier existence hereafter.

157. Q. *What are the other observances which it is considered meritorious for the laity as such to undertake voluntarily to keep?*

A. The *Atthanga Sīla*, or the Eightfold Precept, which embraces the five above enumerated (omitting the word "unlawful" in the third), with three additional; *viz.*:

I observe the precept to abstain from eating at an unseasonable time.

I observe the precept to abstain from dancing, singing, music and unbecoming shows, and from the use of garlands, scents, perfumes, cosmetics, ointments, and ornaments.

I observe the precept to abstain from using high and broad beds.

The seats and couches here referred to are those used by the worldly-minded for the sake of pleasure and sensual enjoyment. The celibate should avoid these.

158. Q. *How would a Buddhist describe true merit?*

A. There is no great merit in any merely outward act; all depends upon the inward motive that provokes the deed.

159. Q. *Give an example?*

A. A rich man may expend lakhs of rupees in building dāgobas or vihāras, in erecting statues of Buddha, in festivals and processions, in feeding priests, in giving alms to the poor, or in planting trees, digging tanks, or constructing rest-houses by the roadside for travellers, and yet have comparatively little merit if it be done for display, or to hear himself praised by men, or for any other selfish motives. But he who does the least of these things with a kind motive, such as love for his fellow-men, gains great merit. A good deed done with a bad motive benefits others, but not the doer. One who approves of a good deed when done by another shares in the merit, *if his sympathy is real, not pretended.* The same rule applies to evil deeds.

160. Q. *But which is said to be the greatest of all meritorious actions?*

A. The *Dhammapada* declares that the merit of disseminating the Dharma, the Law of Righteousness, is greater than that of any other good work.

161. Q. *What books contain all the most excellent wisdom of the Buddha's teachings?*

A. The three collections of books called *Tripitakas* or "*Three Baskets*".

162. Q. *What are the names of the three Pitakas, or groups of books?*

A. The *Vinaya Pitaka,* the *Sutta Pitaka* and the *Abhidhamma Pitaka.*

163. Q. *What do they respectively contain?*

A. The first contains all that pertains to morality and the rules of discipline for the government of the Sangha, or Order; the second contains instructive discourses on ethics applicable to all; the third explains the psychological teachings of the Buddha, including the twenty-four transcendental laws explanatory of the workings of Nature.

164. Q. *Do Buddhists relieve these books to be inspired, or revealed, by a Divine Being?*

A. No; but they revere them as containing all the parts of that most Excellent Law, by the knowing of which man may break through the trammels of *Samsāra.*

165. Q. *In the whole text of the three Pitakas how many words are there?*

A. Dr. Rhys-Davids estimates them at 1,752,800.

166. Q. *When were the Pitakas first reduced to writing?*

A. In 88-76 B.C., under the Sinhalese King, Wattagamini, or three hundred and thirty years after the Paranirvāna of the Buddha.

167. Q. *Have we reason to believe that all the discourses of the Buddha are known to us?*

A. Probably not, and it would be strange if they were. Within the forty-five years of his public life he must have preached many hundreds of discourses. Of these, in times of war and persecution, many must have been lost, many scattered to distant countries, and many mutilated. History says that enemies of the Buddha Dharma burnt piles of our books as high as a coco-nut tree.

168. Q. *Do Buddhists consider the Buddha as one who by his own virtue can save us from the consequence of our individual sins?*

A. Not at all. Man must emancipate himself. Until he does that he will continue being born over and over and over again—the victim of ignorance, the slave of unquenched passions.

169. Q. *What, then, was the Buddha to us, and all other beings?*

A. An all-seeing, all-wise Counsellor; one who discovered the safe path and pointed it out; one who showed the cause of, and the only cure for, human suffering. In pointing to the road, in showing us how to escape dangers, he became our Guide. He is to us like one leading a blind man across a narrow bridge over a swift and deep stream and so saving his life.

170. Q. *If we were to try to represent the whole spirit of the Buddha's doctrine by one word, which word should we choose?*

A. Justice.

171. Q. *Why?*

A. Because it teaches that every man gets, under the operations of unerring KARMA, exactly that reward or punishment which he has deserved, no more and no less. No good deed or bad deed, however trifling, and however secretly committed, escapes the evenly-balanced scales of Karma.

172. Q. *What is Karma?*[*]

A. A causation operating on the moral, as well as on the physical and other planes. Buddhists say there is no miracle in human affairs: what a man sows that he must and will reap.

*Karma is defined as the sum
total of a man's actions. The law of
Cause and Effect is called the *Patice a*

Samuppada   Dhamma.   In the *Anguttara   Nikaya* the   Buddha teaches   that   my   action   is   my possession,   my   action   is   my inheritance, my action is the womb which bears me, my action is my relative, my action is my refuge.

173. Q. *What other good words have been used to express the essence of Buddhism?*

A. Self-culture and universal love.

174. Q. *What doctrine ennobles Buddhism, and gives it its exalted place among the world's religions?*

A.   That   of *Mitta* or *Maitreya*—compassionate   kindness.   The importance of this doctrine is moreover emphasised in the giving of the name "Maitri" (the Compassionate One), to the coming Buddha.

175. Q. *Were all these points of Doctrine that you have explained meditated upon by the Buddha near the Bo-tree?*

A. Yes, these and many more that may be read in the Buddhist Scriptures. The entire system of Buddhism came to his mind during the Great Enlightenment.

176. Q. *How long did the Buddha remain near the Bo-tree?*

A. Forty-nine days.

177. Q. *What do we call the first discourse preached by the Buddha— that which he addressed to his five former companions?*

A.   The *Dhammacakka-ppavattana   sutta*—the   Sūtra   of   the Definition of the Rule of Doctrine.[*]

*After the appearance of the first edition, I received from one of the ablest Pālī scholars of Ceylon, the late L. Corneille Wijesinha, Esq., Mudaliar of Matale, what seems a better rendering of *Dhammacakka-ppavattana* than the one previously given; he makes it "The Establishment of the Reign of Law". Professor Rhys-Davids prefers, "The Foundation of the Kingdom of Righteousness". Mr. Wijesinha writes me: "You may use 'Kingdom of Righteousness,' too, but it savours more of dogmatic theology than of philosophic ethics.*Dhammacakkappavattana suttum* is the discourse entitled 'The Establishment of the Reign of Law'." Having shown this to the High Priest, I am happy to be able to say that he assents to Mr. Wijesinha's rendering.

178. Q. *What subjects were treated by him in this discourse?*

A. The "Four Noble Truths," and the "Noble Eightfold Path". He condemned the extreme physical mortification of the ascetics, on the one hand, and the enjoyment of sensual pleasures on the other; pointing out and recommending the Noble Eightfold Path as the Middle Path.

179. Q. *Did the Buddha hold with idol-worship?*

A. He did not; he opposed it. The worship of gods, demons, trees, etc., was condemned by the Buddha. External worship is a fetter that one has to break if he is to advance higher.

180. Q. *But, do not Buddhists make reverence before the statue of the Buddha, his relics, and the monuments enshrining them?*

A. Yes, but not with the sentiment of the idolater.

181. Q. *What is the difference?*

A. Our Pagan brother not only takes his images as visible representations of his unseen God or gods, but the refined idolater, in worshipping, considers that the idol contains in its substance a portion of the all-pervading divinity.

182. Q. *What does the Buddhist think?*

A. The Buddhist reverences the Buddha's statue and the other things you have mentioned, only as mementoes of the greatest, wisest, most benevolent and compassionate man in this world-period (Kalpa). All races and people preserve, treasure up, and value the relics and mementoes of men and women who have been considered in any way great. The Buddha, to us, seems more to be revered and beloved than any one else, by every human being who knows sorrow.

183. Q. *Has the Buddha himself given us something definite upon this subject?*

A. Certainly. In the *Mahā Pari-Nirvāna Sutta* he says that emancipation is attainable only by leading the Holy life, according to the Noble Eight-fold Path, not by eternal worship (*āmisa pūjā*), nor by adoration of himself, or of another, or of any image.

184. Q. *What was the Buddha's estimate of ceremonialism?*

A. From the beginning, he condemned the observance of ceremonies and other external practices, which only tend to increase our spiritual blindness and our clinging to mere lifeless forms.

185. Q. *What as to controversies?*

A. In numerous discourses he denounced this habit as most pernicious. He prescribed penances for Bhikkhus who waste time and weaken their higher intuitions in wrangling over theories and metaphysical subtleties.

186. Q. *Are charms, incantations, the observance of lucky hours and devil-dancing a part of Buddhism?*

A. They are positively repugnant to its fundamental principles. They are the surviving relics of fetishism and pantheistic and other foreign religions. In the *Brāhmajāta Sutta* the Buddha has categorically described these and other superstitions as Pagan, mean and spurious.[*]

*The mixing of these arts and practices with Buddhism is a sign of deterioration. Their facts and phenomena are real and capable of scientific explanation. They are embraced in the term "magic," but when resorted to, for selfish purposes, attract bad influences about one, and impede spiritual advancement. When employed for harmless and beneficent purposes, such as healing the sick, saving life, etc., the Buddha permitted their use.

187. Q. *What striking contrasts are there between Buddhism and what may be properly called "religions"?*

A. Among others, these: It teaches the highest goodness without a creating God; a continuity of life without adhering to the superstitious and selfish doctrine of an eternal, metaphysical soul-substance that goes out of the body; a happiness without an objective heaven; a method of salvation without a vicarious Saviour; redemption by oneself as the Redeemer, and without rites, prayers, penances, priests or intercessory saints; and a *summum bonum, i.e.,* Nirvāna, attainable in this life and in this world by leading a pure, unselfish life of wisdom and of compassion to all beings.

188. Q. *Specify the two main divisions of "meditation," i.e., of the process by which one extinguishes passion and attains knowledge?*

A. *Samatha* and *Vidarsama*: (1) the attenuation of passion by leading the holy life and by continued effort to subdue the senses; (2) the attainment of supernormal wisdom by reflection: each of which embraces twenty aspects, but I need not here specify them.

189. Q. *What are the four paths or stages of advancement that one may attain to?*

A. (1) Sottāpatti—the beginning or entering into which follows after one's clear perception of the "Four Noble Truths"; (2) Sakardāgāmi—the path of one who has so subjugated lust, hatred and delusion that he need only return once to this world; (3) *Anāgami*—the path of those who have so far conquered self that they need not return to this world; (4) *Arhat*—the path of the holy and worthy Arhat, who is not only free from the necessity of reincarnation, but has capacitated himself to enjoy perfect wisdom, boundless pity for the ignorant and suffering, and measureless love for all beings.

190. Q. *Does popular Buddhism contain nothing but what is true, and in accord with science?*

A. Like every other religion that has existed many centuries, it certainly now contains untruth mingled with truth; ever gold is found mixed with dross. The poetical imagination, the zeal, or the lingering superstition of Buddhist devotees have, in various ages, and in various lands, caused the noble principles of the Buddha's moral doctrines to be coupled more or less with what might be removed to advantage.

191. Q. *When such perversions are discovered, what should be the true Buddhist's earnest desire?*

A. The true Buddhist should be ever ready and anxious to see the false purged away from the true, and to assist, if he can. Three great Councils of the Sangha were held for the express purpose of purging the body of Teachings from all corrupt interpolations.

192. Q. *When?*

A. The first, at Sattapanni cave, just after the death of the Buddha; the second at Valukarama, in Vaisali; the third at Asokarama Vihāra, at Pātaliputra, 235 years after Buddha's decease.

193. Q. *In what discourse does the Buddha himself warn us to expect this perversion of the true Doctrine?*

A. In the *Sanyutta Nikāya*.

194. Q. *Are there any dogmas in Buddhism which we are required to accept on faith?*

A. No: we are earnestly enjoined to accept nothing whatever on faith; whether it be written in books, handed down from our ancestors, or taught by the sages.

195. Q. *Did he himself really teach that noble rule?*

A. Yes. The Buddha has said that we must not believe in a thing said merely because it is said; nor in traditions because they have been handed down from antiquity; nor rumours, as such; nor writings by sages, merely because sages wrote them; nor fancies that we may suspect to have been inspired in us by a Deva (that is, in presumed spiritual inspiration); nor from inferences drawn from some haphazard assumption we may have made; nor because of what seems an analogical necessity; nor on the mere authority of our own teachers or masters.

196. Q. *When, then, must we believe?*

A. We are to believe when the writing doctrine or saying is corroborated by our own reason and consciousness. "For this," says he in concluding, "I taught you not to believe merely because you have heard, but when you believed of your own consciousness, then to act accordingly and abundantly." (See the *Kālāma Sutta* of the *Anguttara Nikāya*, and the *Mahā Pari Nirvāna Sutta*.)

197. Q. *What does the Buddha call himself?*

A. He says that he and the other Buddhas are only "preachers" of truth who point out the way: we ourselves must make the effort.

198. Q. *Where is this said?*

A. In the *Dhammapada*, Chapter xx.

199. Q. *Does Buddhism countenance hypocrisy?*

A. The Dhammapada says: "Like a beautiful flower full of colour without scent the fine words of him who does not act accordingly are fruitless."

200. Q. *Does Buddhism teach us to return evil for evil?*

A. In the *Dhammapada* the Buddha said: "If a man foolishly does me wrong, I will return to him the protection of my ungrudging love; the more evil comes from him, the more good shall go from me." This is the path followed by the Arhat.[*] To return evil for evil is positively forbidden in Buddhism.

* A Buddhist ascetic who, by a prescribed course of practice, has attained to a superior state of spiritual and intellectual development. Arhats may be divided into the two general groups of the *Samathayanika* and *Sukkha Vipassaka*. The former have destroyed their passions, and fully developed their intellectual capacity or mystical insight; the latter have equally conquered passion, but not acquired the superior mental powers. The former can work phenomena, the latter cannot. The Arhat of the former class, when fully developed, is no longer a prey to the delusions of the senses, nor the slave of passion or mortal frailty. *He penetrates to the root of whatsoever subject his mind is applied to* without following the slow processes of reasoning. His self-conquest is complete; and in place of the emotion and desire which vex and

enthral the ordinary man, he is lifted up into a condition which is best expressed in the term "Nirvānic". There is in Ceylon a popular misconception that the attainment of Arhatship is now impossible; that the Buddha had himself prophesied that the power would die out in one millennium after his death. This rumour—and the similar one that is everywhere heard in India, *viz.*, that this being the dark cycle of the *Kali Yuga*, the practice of Yoga Vidyā, or sublime spiritual science, is impossible—I ascribe to the ingenuity of those who should be as pure and (to use a non-Buddhistic but very convenient term) psychically wise as were their predecessors, but are not, and who therefore seek an excuse! The Buddha taught quite the contrary idea. In the *Nīga Nikāya* he said: "Hear, Subbhadra! The world will never be without Arhats if the ascetics (Bhikkhus) in my congregations *well and truly keep my precepts.*" (*Imeccha Subhaddabhikkhu samma vihareiyum asunno loko Arahantehiassa.*)

201. Q. *Does it encourage cruelty?*

A. No, indeed. In the Five Precepts and in many of his discourses, the Buddha teaches us to be merciful to all beings, to try and make them happy, to love them all, to abstain from taking life, or consenting to it, or encouraging its being done.

202. Q. *In which discourse is this stated?*

A. The *Dhammika Sutta* says: "Let him (the householder) not destroy, or cause to be destroyed, any life at all, or *sanction the act of those who do so.* Let him refrain from even hurting any creature."[*]

*Kolb, in his *History of Culture*, says: "It is Buddhism we have to thank for the sparing of prisoners of war, who heretofore had been slain; also for the discontinuance of the carrying away into captivity of the inhabitants of conquered lands."

203. Q. *Does it approve of drunkenness?*

A. In his *Dhammika Sutta* we are warned against drinking liquors, causing others to drink, or sanctioning the acts of those who drink.[*]

* The fifth Sīla has reference to the mere taking of intoxicants and stupefying drugs, which leads ultimately to drunkenness.

204. Q. *To what are we told that drunkenness leads?*

A. To demerit, crime, insanity, and ignorance—which is the chief cause of rebirth.

205. Q. *What does Buddhism teach about marriage?*

A. Absolute chastity being a condition of full spiritual development, is most highly commended; but a marriage to one wife and fidelity to her is recognised as a kind of chastity. Polygamy was censured by the Buddha as involving ignorance and promoting lust.

206. Q. *In what discourse?*

A. The *Anguttara Nikāya*, Chapter iv, 55.

207. Q. *What does it teach as to the duty of parents to children?*

A. They should restrain them from vice, train them in virtue; have them taught arts and sciences; provide them with suitable wives and husbands, and give them their inheritance.

208. Q. What is the duty of children?

A. To support their parents when old or needy; perform family duties incumbent on them; guard their property; make themselves worthy to be their heirs, and when they are gone, honour their memory.

209. Q. *What of pupils to the teacher?*

A. To show him respect; minister to him; obey him; supply his wants; attend to his instruction.

210. Q. *What of husband to wife?*

A. To cherish her; treat her with respect and kindness; be faithful to her; cause her to be honoured by others; provide her with suitable ornaments and clothes.

211. Q. *What of the wife to her husband?*

A. To show affection to him; order her household aright; be hospitable to guests; be chaste; be thrifty; show skill and diligence in all things.

212. Q. Where are these precepts taught?

A. In the Sigālovāda Sutta.

213. Q. Do riches help a man to future happiness?

A. The Dhammapada says: "One is the road that leads to wealth, another the road that leads to Nirvāna."

214. Q. Does that mean that no rich man can attain Nirvāna?

A. That depends on which he loves most. If he uses his wealth for the benefit of mankind—for the suffering, the oppressed, the ignorant—then his wealth aids him to acquire merit.

215. Q. But if the contrary?

A. But if he loves and greedily hoards money for the sake of its possession, then it weakens his moral sense, prompts him to crime, brings curses upon him in this life, and their effects are felt in the next birth.

216. Q. *What says the "Dhammapada" about ignorance?*

A. That it is a taint worse than all taints that a man can put upon himself.

217. Q. *What does it say about uncharitableness towards others?*

A. That the fault of others is easily perceived, but that of oneself difficult to perceive; a man winnows his neighbour's faults like chaff, but his own fault he hides, as a cheat hides the bad die from the gambler.

218. Q. *What advice does the Buddha give us as to man's duty to the poor?*

A. He says that a man's net income should be divided into four parts, of which one should be devoted to philanthropic objects.

219. Q. *What five occupations are said to be low and base?*

A. Selling liquor, selling animals for slaughter, selling poison, selling murderous weapons, and dealing in slaves.

220. Q. *Who are said to be incapable of progress in spirituality?*

A. The killers of father, mother, and holy Arhats; Bhikkhus who sow discord in the Sangha; those who attempt to injure the person of a Buddha; those who hold extremely nihilistic views as to the future existence; and those who are extremely sensual.

121. Q. *Does Buddhism specify places or conditions of torment into which a bad man's Karma draws him on leaving this life?*

A. Yes. They are: Sanjīva; Kālasūtra; Sanghāta; Raurava; Mahā-Raurava Tāpa; Pratāpa; Avīchi.

222. Q. *Is the torment eternal?*

A. Certainly not. Its duration depends on a man's Karma.

223. Q. *Does Buddhism declare that non-believers in Buddha will of necessity be damned for their unbelief?*

A. No; by good deeds they may enjoy a limited term of happiness before being drawn into rebirth by their unexhausted *tanhā*. To escape rebirth, one must tread the Noble Eight-fold Path.

224. Q. *What is the spiritual status of woman among Buddhists?*

A. According to our religion they are on a footing of perfect equality with men. "Woman," says the Buddha, in the *Chullavedalla Sutta*, "may attain the highest path of holiness that is open to man—Arhatship."

225. Q. *What does a modern critic say about the effect of Buddhism on woman?*

A. That "it has done more for the happiness and enfranchisement of woman than any other creed" (Sir Lepel Griffin).

226. Q. *What did the Buddha teach about caste?*

A. That one does not become of any caste, whether Pariah, the lowest, or Brāhmana the highest, by birth, but by deeds. "By deeds," said He, "one becomes an outcast, by deeds one becomes a Brāhmana" (See *Vassala Sutta*).

227. Q. *Tell me a story to illustrate this?*

A. Ananda, passing by a well, was thirsty and asked Prakrti, a girl of the Mātanga, or Pariah, caste, to give him water. She said she was of such low caste that he would become contaminated by taking water from her hand. But Ananda replied: "I ask not for caste but for water"; and the Mātanga girl's heart was glad and she gave him to drink. The Buddha blessed her for it.

228. Q. *What did the Buddha say in "Vasala Sutta" about a man of the Pariah Sopāka caste?*

A. That by his merits he reached the highest fame; that many Khattiyas (Kshattriyas) and Brāhmanas went to serve him; and that after death he was born in the Brāhma-world: while there are many Brāhmanas who for their evil deeds are born in hell.

229. Q. Does Buddhism teach the immortality of the soul?

A. It considers "soul" to be a word used by the ignorant to express a false idea. If everything is subject to change, then man is included, and every material part of him must change. That which is subject to change is not permanent: so there can be no immortal survival of a changeful thing.[*]

* The "soul" here criticised is the equivalent of the Greek *psuche*. The word "material" covers other states of matter than that of the physical body.

230. Q. *What is so objectionable in this word "soul"?*

A. The idea associated with it that man can be an entity separated from all other entities, and from the existence of the whole of the Universe. This idea of separateness is unreasonable, not provable by logic, nor supported by science.

231. Q. *Then there is no separate "I," nor can we say "my" this or that?*

A. Exactly so.

232. Q. *If the idea of a separate human "soul" is to be rejected, what is it in man which gives him the impression of having a permanent personality?*

A. *Tanhā*, or the unsatisfied desire for existence. The being having done that for which he must be rewarded or punished in future, and having *Tanhā*, will have a rebirth through the influence of Karma.

233. Q. *What is it that is born?*

A. A new aggregation of Skandhas, or personality[*] caused by the last generative thought of the dying person.

* Upon reflection, I have substituted "personality" for "individuality" as written in the first edition. The successive appearances upon one or many earths, or "descents into generation," of the *tanhaically*-coherent parts (*Skandhas*) of a certain being are a succession of personalities. In each birth the *personality* differs from that of the previous, or next succeeding birth. Karma the *deus ex machina*, masks (or shall we say reflects?) itself, now in the personality of a sage, again as an artisan, and so on throughout the string of births. But though personalities ever shift, the one line of life along which they are strung like beads, runs unbroken, it is ever *that particular line*, never any other. It is therefore individual—an individual vital undulation—which is careering through the objective side of Nature, under the impulse of Karma and the creative direction of Tanhā and persists through many cyclic changes. Professor Rhys-Davids calls that which passes from personality to personality along the individual chain, "character" or "doing". Since "character" is not a mere metaphysical abstraction, but the sum of one's mental qualities and moral propensities, would it not help to dispel what Professor Rhys-Davids calls "the desperate expedient of a mystery" (*Buddhism*, p. 101), if we regarded the life-undulation as individuality and each of its series of natal manifestations as a separate personality? We *must* have two words to distinguish between the concepts, and I find none so clear and expressive as the two I have chosen. The perfected individual, Buddhistically speaking, is a Buddha, I should say; for a Buddha is but the rare flower of humanity, without the least supernatural admixture. And, as countless generations—"four *asankhyyas* and a hundred thousand cycles" (Fausboll and Rhys-David's *Buddhist Birth Stories*, No. 13)— are required to develop a man into a Buddha, and *the iron will to become one runs throughout all the successive births*, what shall we call that which thus

wills and perseveres? Character, or individuality? An individuality, but partly manifested in any one birth, built up of fragments from all the births.

The denial of "Soul" by Buddha (see *Sanyutta Nikāya*, the *Sutta Pitaka*) points to the prevalent delusive belief in an independent personality; an entity, which after one birth would go to a fixed place or state where, as a perfect entity, it could eternally enjoy or suffer. And what he shows is that the "I am I" consciousness is, as regards permanency, logically impossible, since its elementary constituents constantly change and the "I" of one birth differs from the "I" of every other birth. But everything that I have found in Buddhism accords with the theory of a gradual evolution of the perfected man—*viz.*, a Buddha—through numberless natal experiences. And in the consciousness of that individual who, at the end of a given chain of births, attains Buddhahood, or who succeeds in attaining the fourth stage of Dhyāna, or mystic self-development, in any of his births anterior to the final one, the scenes of all these serial births are perceptible. In the *Jātakat-thavannana*—so well translated by Professor Rhys-Davids—an expression continually recurs which, I think, rather supports such an idea, *viz.*: "Then the Blessed One *made manifest an occurrence hidden by change of birth*," or "that which had been hidden by," etc. Early Buddhism then clearly held to a permanency of records in the Ākāsha, and the potential capacity of man to read the same when he has evolved to the stage of true individual enlightenment. At death, and in convulsions and trance, the *javana chittā* is transferred to the object last created by the desires. The will to live brings all thoughts into objectivity.

234. Q. *How many Skandhas are there?*

A. Five.

235. Q. *Name the five Skandhas?*

A. Rūpa, Vedanā, Saññā, Samkhārā, *and* Viññāna.

236. Q. Briefly explain what they are?

A. Rūpa, material qualities; *Vedanā*, sensation; *Saññā*, abstract ideas; *Samkhārā*, tendencies of mind; *Viññāna*, mental powers, or consciousness. Of these we are formed; by them we are conscious of existence; and through them communicate with the world about us.

237. Q. *To what cause must we attribute the differences in the combination of the five Skandhas which make every individual differ from every other individual?*

A. To the ripened Karma of the individual in his preceding births.

238. Q. *What is the force of energy that is at work, under the guidance of Karma, to produce the new being?*

A. Tanhā—the will to *live*.[*]

* The student may profitably consult Schopenhauer in this connection. Arthur Schopenhauer, a modern German philosopher of the most eminent ability, taught that "the Principle or Radical, of Nature, and of all her objects, the human body included, is, intrinsically what we ourselves are the most conscious of in our own body, *viz.*, Will. Intellect is a secondary capacity of the primary will, a function of the brain in which this will reflects itself as Nature and object and body, as in a mirror... Intellect is secondary, but may lead, in saints, to a complete renunciation of will, as far as it urges "life" and is then extinguished in Nirvāna (L. A. Sanders in *The Theosophist* for May 1882, p. 213).

239. Q. *Upon what is the doctrine of rebirths founded?*

A. Upon the perception that perfect justice, equilibrium and adjustment are inherent in the universal system of Nature. Buddhists do not believe that one life—even though it were extended to one hundred or five hundred years—is long enough for the reward or punishment of a man's deeds. The great circle of rebirths will be more or less quickly run through according to the preponderating purity or impurity of the several lives of the individual.

240. Q. *Is this new aggregation of Skandhas—this new personality—the same being as that in the previous birth, whose Tanhā has brought it into existence?*

A. In one sense it is a new being; in another it is not. In Pālī it is— "*nacha so nacha añño*" which means not the same nor yet another. During this life the *Skandhas* are constantly changing;[*] and while the man A. B., of forty, is identical, as regards personality, with the youth A. B., of eighteen, yet, by the continual waste and reparation of his body, and change of mind and character, he is a different being. Nevertheless, the man in his old age justly reaps the reward of suffering consequent upon his thoughts and actions at every previous stage of his life. So the new being of a rebirth, being the same individuality as before, but with a changed form, or new aggregation of *Skandhas*, justly reaps the consequences of his actions and thoughts in the previous existence.

* Physiologically speaking, man's body is completely changed every seven years.

241. Q. *But the aged man remembers the incidents of his youth, despite his being physically and mentally changed. Why, then, is not the recollection of past lives brought over by us from our last birth, into the present birth?*

A. Because memory is included within the *Skandhas*; and the *Skandhas* having changed with the new reincarnation, a new memory, the record of of that particular existence, develops. Yet the record or reflection of all the past earth-lives must survive; for, when Prince Siddhārtha became Buddha, the full sequence of his previous births was seen by him. If their several incidents had left no trace behind, this could not have been so, as there would have been nothing for him to see. And any one who attains to the fourth state of *Dhyāna* (psychical insight) can thus retrospectively trace the line of his lives.

242. Q. *What is the ultimate point towards which tend all these series of changes in form?*

A. Nirvāna.

243. Q. *Does Buddhism teach that we should do good with the view of reaching Nirvāna?*

A. No; that would be as absolute selfishness as though the reward hoped for had been money, a throne, or any other sensual enjoyment. Nirvāna cannot be so reached, and the unwise speculator is foredoomed to disappointment.

244. Q. *Please make it a little clearer?*

A. Nirvāna is the synonym of unselfishness, the entire surrender of selfhood to truth. The ignorant man aspires to nirvānic happiness without the least idea of its nature. Absence of selfishness is Nirvāna. Doing good with the view to getting results, or leading the holy life with the object of gaining heavenly happiness, is not the Noble Life that the Buddha enjoined. Without hope of reward the Noble Life should be lived, and that is the highest life. The nirvānic state can be attained while one is living on this earth.

245. Q. *Name the ten great obstacles to advancement, called Sanyojanas, the Fetters?*

A. Delusion of self (*Sakkāya-ditthi*); Doubt (*Vicikicchā*); Dependence on superstitious rites (*Sīlabbata-parāmāsa*); Sensuality, bodily passions (*Kāma*); Hatred, ill-feeling (*Patigha*); Love of life on earth (*Rūparāga*); Desire for life in a heaven (*Arūparāga*); Pride (*Māna*); Self-righteousness (Uddhacca); Ignorance (*Avijjā*).

246. Q. *To become an Arhat, how many of these fetters must be broken?*

A. All.

247. Q. *What are the five Nirwāranas or Hindrances?*

A. Greed, Malice, Sloth, Pride, and Doubt.

248. Q. *Why do we see this minute division of feelings, impulses, workings of the mind, obstacles and aids to advancement so much used in the Buddha's teachings? It is very confusing to a beginner.*

A. It is to help us to obtain knowledge of ourselves, by training our minds to think out every subject in detail. By following out this system of self-examination, we come finally to acquire knowledge and see truth as it is. This is the course taken by every wise teacher to help his pupil's mind to develop.

249. Q. *How many of the Buddha's disciples were specially renowned for their superior qualities?*

A. There are eighty so distinguished. They are called the Asīti Mahā Sāvakas.

250. Q. *What did the Buddha's wisdom embrace?*

A. He knew the nature of the Knowable and the Unknowable, the Possible and the Impossible, the cause of Merit and Demerit; he could read the thoughts of all beings; he knew the laws of Nature, the illusions of the senses and the means to suppress desires; he could distinguish the birth and rebirth of individuals, and other things.

251. Q. *What do we call the basic principle on which the whole of the Buddha's teaching is constructed?*

A. It is called Paticca Samuppāda.[*]

* This fundamental or basic principle may be designated in Pālī, *Nidāna*—chain of causation or, literally, "Origination of dependence". Twelve *Nidānas* are specified, *viz.*: *Avijjā*—ignorance of the truth of natural religion; *Samkhāra*—causal action, karma; *Viññana*—consciousness of personality, the "I am I"; *Nāma rūpa*—name and form; *Salayatana*—six senses; *Phassa*—contact, *Vedanā*—feeling, *Tanhā*—desire for enjoyment; *Upādāna*—clinging, *Bhava*—individualising existence; *Jāti*—birth, caste; *Jarā, narana, sokaparidesa, dukkha, domanassa, upāyāsa*—decay, death, grief, lamentation, despair.

252. Q. *Is it easily grasped?*

A. It is most difficult; in fact, the full meaning and extent of it is beyond the capacity of such as are not perfectly developed.

253. Q. *What said the great commentator Buddha Ghosha about it?*

A. That even he was as helpless in this vast ocean of thought as one who is drifting on the ocean of waters.

254. Q. *Then why should the Buddha say, in the Parinibbāna Sutta, that he "has no such thing as the closed fist of a teacher, who keeps something back"? If his whole teaching was open to every one's comprehension why should so great and learned a man as Buddha Ghosha declare it so hard to understand?*

A. The Buddha evidently meant that he taught everything freely; but equally certain is it that the real basis of the Dharma can only be understood by him who has perfected his powers of comprehension. It is, therefore, incomprehensible to common, unenlightened persons.

255. Q. *How does the teaching of the Buddha support this view?*

A. The Buddha looked into the heart of each person, and preached to suit the individual temperament and spiritual development of the hearer.

PART III. THE SANGHA

256. Q. *How do Buddhist Bhikkhus differ from the priests of other religions?*

A. In other religions the priests claim to be intercessors between men and God, to help to obtain pardon of sins; the Buddhist Bhikkhus do not acknowledge or expect anything from a divine power.

257. Q. *But why then was it worth while to create this Order, or Brotherhood, or Society, apart from the whole body of the people, if they were not to do what other religious orders do?*

A. The object in view was to cause the most virtuous, intelligent, unselfish and spiritually-minded persons to withdraw from the social surroundings where their sensual and other selfish desires were naturally strengthened, devote their lives to the acquisition of the highest wisdom, and fit themselves to teach and guide others out of the pleasant path leading towards misery, into the harder path that leads to true happiness and final liberation.

258. Q. *Besides the Eight, what two additional observances are obligatory upon the Bhikkhus?*

A. I observe the precept to abstain from dancing, singing and unbecoming shows.

I observe the precept to abstain from receiving gold or silver.

The whole *Dasa*, or *Bhikkhu Sīla* or Ten Precepts, are binding on *all* Bhikkhus and *Samaneras*, or novices, but optional with lay devotees.

The *Atthanga Sīla* are for those who aspire to higher stages beyond the heavenly regions,[*] aspirants after Nirvāna.

* The Upāsaka and Upāsika observe these on the Buddhist *Uposatha* (Sabbath) days (in Skr. *Upavasata*). They are the 8th, 14th and 15th days of each half lunar month.

259. Q. *Are there separate Rules and Precepts for the guidance and discipline of the Order?*

A. Yes: there are 250, but all come under the following four heads:

Principal Disciplinary Rules {*Pātimokkha Samvara Sīla*).

Observances for the repression of the senses (*Indriya Samvara Sīla*).

Regulations for justly procuring and using food, diet, robes, etc., (*Paccaya Sannissita Sīla*).

Directions for leading an unblemished life (*Ajivapari Suddha Sīla*).

45

260. Q. *Enumerate some crimes and offences that Bhikkhus are particularly prohibited from committing?*

A. Real Bhikkhus abstain from:

Destroying the life of beings;

Stealing;

False exhibition of "occult" powers to deceive anybody;

Sexual intercourse;

Falsehood;

The use of intoxicating liquors, and eating at unseasonable times;

Dancing, singing, and unbecoming shows;

Using garlands, scents, perfumes, etc.;

Using high and broad beds, couches, or seats; receiving presents of gold, silver, raw grain and meat, women, and maidens, slaves, cattle, elephants, etc.;

Defaming;

Using harsh and reproachful language;

Idle talk;

Reading and hearing fabulous stories and tales;

Carrying messages to and from laymen;

Buying and selling;

Cheating, bribing, deception, and fraud;

Imprisoning, plundering, and threatening others;

The practice of certain specified magical arts and sciences, such as fortune-telling, astrological predictions, palmistry, and other sciences, that go under the name of magic. Any of these would retard the progress of one who aimed at the attainment of Nirvāna.

261. Q. *What are the duties of Bhikkhus to the laity?*

A. Generally, to set them an example of the highest morality; to teach and instruct them; to preach and expound the Law; to recite the *Paritta* (comforting texts) to the sick, and publicly in times of public calamity, when requested to do so; and unceasingly to exhort the people to virtuous actions. They should dissuade them from vice; be compassionate and tender-hearted, and seek to promote the welfare of all beings.

262. Q. *What are the rules for admission into the Order?*

A. The candidate is not often taken before his tenth year; he must have the consent of his parents; be free from leprosy, boils, consumption and fits; be a free man; have no debts; and must not be a criminal or deformed or in the royal service.

263. Q. *As a novice what is he called?*

A. *Samanera*, a pupil.[*] * The relationship to his Guru, or teacher, is almost like that of godson to godfather among Christians, only more real, for the teacher becomes father, mother, family and all to him.

264. Q. *At what age can a Samanera be ordained as* Sramana— *monk?*

A. Not before his twentieth year.

265. Q. When ready for ordination what happens?

A. At a meeting of Bhikkhus he is presented by a Bhikkhu as his proposer, who reports that he is qualified, and the candidate says: "I ask the Sangha, Reverend Sirs, for the *Upasampada* (ordination) ceremony, etc."

His introducer then recommends that he be admitted. He is then accepted.

266. Q. *What then?*

A. He puts on the robes and repeats the Three Refuges {*Tisarana)* and Ten Precepts (*Dasa Sīla*.)

267. Q. *What are the two essentials to be observed?*

A. Poverty and Chastity. A Bhikkhu before ordination must possess eight things, *viz*., his robes, a girdle for his loins, a begging-bowl, water-strainer, razor, needle, fan, sandals. Within limitations strictly specified in the Vināya, he may hold certain other properties.

268. Q. *What about the public confession of faults?*

A. Once every fortnight, a *Patimokka* (Disburdenment) ceremony is performed, when every Bhikkhu confesses to the assembly such faults as he has committed and takes such penances as may be prescribed.

269. Q. *What daily routine must he follow?*

A. He rises before daylight, washes, sweeps the vihāra, sweeps around the Bo-tree that grows near every vihāra, brings the drinking-water for the day and filters it; retires for meditation, offers flowers before the dāgoba, or relic-mound, or before the Bo-tree; then takes his begging-bowl and goes from house to house collecting food—which he must not ask for, but receive in his bowl as given voluntarily by the householders. He returns, bathes his feet and eats, after which he resumes meditation.

270. Q. *Must we believe that there is no merit in the offering of flowers (mala pūjā) as an act of worship?*

A. That act itself is without merit as a mere formality; but if one offers a flower as the sweetest, purest expression of heartfelt reverence for a holy being, then, indeed, is the offering an act of ennobling worship.

271. Q. *What next does the Bhikkhu do?*

A. He pursues his studies. At sunset he again sweeps the sacred places, lights a lamp, listens to the instructions of his superior, and confesses to him any fault he may have committed.

272. Q. *Upon what are his four earnest meditations (Sati-patthāna) made?*

A. 1. On the body, Kayānapassānā.

2. On the feeling, Vedanānupassānā.

3. On the mind, Chittānnpassānā.

4. On the doctrine, Dhammānupassānā.

273. Q. *What is the aim of the four Great Efforts (Sammappadhānā)?*

A. To suppress one's animal desires and grow in goodness.

274. Q. *For the perception by the Bhikkhu of the highest truth, is reason said to be the best, or intuition?*

A. Intuition—a mental state in which any desired truth is instantaneously grasped.

275. Q. *And when can that development be reached?*

A. When one, by the practice of Jñāna, comes to its fourth stage of unfolding.

276. Q. *Are we to believe that in the final stage of Jñāna, and in the condition called Samādhi, the mind is a blank and thought is arrested?*

A. Quite the contrary. It is then that one's consciousness is most intensely active, and one's power to gain knowledge correspondingly vast.

277. Q. *Try to give me a simile?*

A. In the ordinary waking state one's view of knowledge is as limited as the sight of a man who walks on a road between high hills; in the higher consciousness of Jñāna and *Samādhi* it is like the sight of the eagle poised in the upper sky and overlooking a whole country.

278. Q. *What do our books say about the Buddha's use of this faculty?*

A. They tell us that it was his custom, every morning, to glance over the world and, by his divine (clairvoyant) sight, see where there were persons ready to receive the truth. He would then contrive, if possible, that it should reach them. When persons visited him he would look into their minds, read their secret motives, and then preach to them according to their needs.

PART IV. THE RISE AND SPREAD OF BUDDHISM

279. Q. *As regards the number its followers, how does Buddhism at this date compare with the other chief religions?*

A. The followers of the Buddha Dharma outnumber those of every other religion.

280. Q. *What is the estimated number?*

A. About five hundred millions (5,000 lakhs or 500 crores): this is five-thirteenths, or not quite half, of the estimated population of the globe.

281. Q. *Have many great battles been fought and many countries conquered; has much human blood been spilt to spread the Buddha Dharma?*

A. History does not record one of those cruelties and crimes as having been committed to propagate our religion. So far as we know, it has not caused the spilling of a drop of blood. (See footnote *ante*—Professor Kolb's testimony.)

282. Q. *What, then, is the secret of its wonderful spread?*

A. It can be nothing else than its intrinsic excellence: its self-evident basis of truth, its sublime moral teaching, and its sufficiency for all human needs.

283. Q. *How has it been propagated?*

A. The Buddha, during the forty-five years of his life as a Teacher, travelled widely in India and preached the Dharma. He sent his wisest and best disciples to do the same throughout India.

284. Q. *When did He send for his pioneer missionaries?*

A. On the full-moon day of the month *Wap* (October).

285. Q. *What did he tell them?*

A. He called them together and said: "Go forth, Bhikkhus, go and preach the law to the world. Work for the good of others as well as for your own.... Bear ye the glad tidings to every man. Let no two of you take the same way."

286. Q. *How long before the Christian era did this happen?*

A. About six centuries.

287. Q. *What help did Kings give?*

A. Besides the lower classes, great Kings, Rājās and Mahārājās were converted and gave their influence to spread the religion.

288. Q. *What about pilgrims?*

A. Learned pilgrims came in different centuries to India and carried back with them books and teachings to their native lands. So, gradually, whole nations forsook their own faiths and became Buddhists.

289. Q. *To whom, more than to any other person, is the world indebted for the permanent establishment of Buddha's religion?*

A. To the Emperor Ashoka, surnamed the Great, sometimes Piyadāsi, sometimes Dharmāshoka. He was the son of Bindusāra, King of Magadha, arid grandson of Chandragupta, who drove the Greeks out of India.

290. Q. *When did he reign?*

A. In the third century B.C., about two centuries after the Buddha's time. Historians disagree as to his exact date, but not very greatly.

291. Q. *What made him great?*

A. He was the most powerful monarch in Indian history, as warrior and as statesman; but his noblest characteristics were his love of truth and justice, tolerance of religious differences, equity of government, kindness to the sick, to the poor, and to animals. His name is revered from Siberia to Ceylon.

292. Q. *Was he born a Buddhist?*

A. No, he was converted in the tenth year after his anointment as King, by Nigrodha Samanera, an Arhat.

293. Q. *What did he do for Buddhism?*

A. He drove out bad Bhikkhus, encouraged good ones, built monasteries and dāgobas everywhere, established gardens, opened hospitals for men and animals, convened a council at Patna to revise and re-establish the Dharma, promoted female religious education, and sent embassies to five Greek kings, his allies, and to all the sovereigns of India, to preach the doctrines of the Buddha. It was he who built the monuments at Kapilavastu, Buddha Gāya, Isipatana and Kusinārā, our four chief places of pilgrimage, besides thousands more.

294. Q. *What absolute proofs exist as to his noble character?*

A. Within recent years there have been discovered, in all parts of India, fourteen Edicts of his, inscribed on living rocks, and eight on pillars erected by his orders. They fully prove him to have been one of the wisest and most high-minded sovereigns who ever lived.

29.5. Q. *What character do these inscriptions give to Buddhism?*

A. They show it to be a religion of noble tolerance, of universal brotherhood, of righteousness and justice. It has no taint of selfishness, sectarianism or intolerance. They have done more than anything else to win for it the respect in which it is now held by the great pandits of western countries.

296. Q. *What most precious gift did Dharmāshoka make to Buddhism?*

A. He gave his beloved son, Mahinda, and daughter, Sanghamitta, to the Order, and sent them to Ceylon to introduce the religion.

297. Q. *Is this fact recorded in the history of Ceylon?*

A. Yes, it is all recorded in the Mahāvansa, by the keepers of the royal records, who were then living and saw the missionaries.

298. Q. *Is there some proof of Sanghamitta's mission still visible?*

A. Yes; she brought with her to Ceylon a branch of the very Bodhi tree under which the Buddha sat when he became Enlightened, and it is still growing.

299. Q. *Where?*

A. At Annrādhapura. The history of it has been officially preserved to the present time. Planted in 306 B.C., it is the oldest historical tree in the world.

300. Q. *Who was the reigning sovereign at that time?*

A. Dēvanampiyatissa. His consort, Queen Anula, had invited Sanghamitta to come and establish the Bhikkhuni branch of the Order.

301. Q. *Who came with Sanghamitta?*

A. Many other Bhikkhunis. She, in due time, admitted the Queen and many of her ladies, together with five hundred virgins, into the Order.

302. Q. *Can we trace the effects of the foreign work of the Emperor Ashoka's missionaries?*

A. His son and daughter introduced Buddhism into Ceylon: his monks gave it to the whole of Northern India, to fourteen Indian nations outside its boundaries, and to five Greek kings, his allies, with whom he made treaties to admit his religious preachers.

303. Q. *Can you name them?*

A. ANTIOCHUS of Syria, PTOLEMY of Egypt, ANTIGONUS of Macedon, MARGAS of Cyrene, and ALEXANDER of Epiros.

04. Q. *Where do we learn this?*

A. From the Edicts themselves of Ashoka the Great, inscribed by him on rocks and stone pillars, which are still standing and can be seen by everybody who chooses to visit the places.

305. Q. *Through what western religious brotherhoods did the Buddha Dharma mingle itself with western thought?*

A. Through the sects of the Therapeuts of Egypt and the Essenes of Palestine.

306. Q. *When were Buddhist books first introduced into China?*

A. As early as the second or third century B.C. Five of Dharmāshoka's monks are said—in the Samanta Pasādika and the Sārattha Dīpanī—two Pālī books—to have been sent to the five divisions of China.

307. Q. *Whence and when did it reach Korea?*

A. From China, in the year A. D. 372.

308. Q. *Whence and when did it reach Japan?*

A. From Korea, in A. D. 552.

309. Q. *Whence and when did it reach Cochin China, Formosa, Java, Mongolia, Yorkand, Balk, Bokhara, Afghanistan and other Central Asian countries?*

A. Apparently in the fourth and fifth centuries A.D.

310. Q. *From Ceylon, whither and when did it spread?*

A. To Burma, in A.D. 450, and thence gradually into Arakan, Kamboya and Pegu. In the seventh century (A.D. 638) it spread to Siam, where it is now, as it has been always since then, the State religion.

311. Q. *From Kashmir, where else did it spread besides to China?*

A. To Nepāl and Tibet.

312. Q. Why is it that Buddhism, which was once the prevailing religion throughout India, is now almost extinct there?

A. Buddhism was at first pure and noble, the very teaching of the Tathagata; its Sangha were virtuous and observed the Precepts; it won all hearts and spread joy through many nations, as the morning light sends life through the flowers. But after some centuries, bad Bhikkhus got ordination (*Upasampada*) the Sangha became rich, lazy, and sensual, the Dharma was corrupted, and the Indian nation abandoned it.

313. Q. *Did anything happen about the ninth or tenth century A.D. to hasten its downfall?*

A. Yes.

314. Q. *Anything besides the decay of spirituality, the corruption of the Sangha, and the reaction of the populace from a higher ideal of man to unintelligent idolatry?*

A. Yes. It is said that the Mussalmāns invaded, overran and conquered large areas of India; everywhere doing their utmost to stamp out our religion.

315. Q. *What cruel acts are they charged with doing?*

A. They burnt, pulled down or otherwise destroyed our vihāras, slaughtered our Bhikkhus, and consumed with fire our religious books.

316. Q. *Was our literature completely destroyed in India?*

A. No. Many Bhikkhus fled across the borders into Tibet and other safe places of refuge, carrying their books with them.

317. Q. *Have any traces of these books been recently discovered?*

A. Yes. Rai Bhādur Sarat Chandra Dās, C.I.E., a noted Bengali pandit, saw hundreds of them in the vihāra libraries of Tibet, brought copies of some of the most important back with him, and is now employed by the Government of India in editing and publishing them.

318. Q. *In which country have we reason to believe the sacred books of primitive Buddhism have been best preserved and least corrupted?*

A. Ceylon. The *Encyclopaedia Britannica* says that in this island Buddhism has, for specified reasons, "retained almost its pristine purity to modern times".

319. Q. *Has any revision of the text of the Pitakas been made in modern times?*

A. Yes. A careful revision of the Vināya Pitaka was made in Ceylon in the year A.D. 1875, by a convention of the most learned Bhikkhus, under the presidency of H. Sumangala, Pradhāna Sthavīra.

320. Q. *Has there been any friendly intercourse in the interest of Buddhism between the peoples of the Southern and those of the Northern Buddhist countries?*

A. In the year A.D. 1891, a successful attempt was made to get the Pradhāna Nayakas of the two great divisions to agree to accept fourteen propositions as embodying fundamental Buddhistic beliefs recognised and taught by both divisions. These propositions, drafted by Colonel Olcott, were carefully translated into Burmese, Sinhalese and Japanese, discussed one by one, unanimously adopted and signed by the chief monks, and published in January 1892.

321. Q. *With what good result?*

A. As the result of the good understanding now existing, a number of Japanese bhikkhus and samaneras have been sent to Ceylon and India to study Pālī and Samskrt.

322. Q. *Are there signs that the Buddha Dharma is growing in favour in non-Buddhistic countries?*[See Appendix.]

A. There are. Translations of our more valuable books are appearing, many articles in reviews, magazines and newspapers are being published, and excellent original treatises by distinguished writers are coming from the press. Moreover, Buddhist and non-Buddhist lecturers are publicly discoursing on Buddhism to large audiences in western countries. The Shin Shu sect of Japanese Buddhists have actually opened missions at Honolulu, San Francisco, Sacramento and other American places.

323. Q. *What two leading ideas of ours are chiefly taking hold upon the western mind?*

A. Those of Karma and Reincarnation. The rapidity of their acceptance is very surprising.

324. Q. *What is believed to be the explanation of this?*

A. Their appeals to the natural instinct of justice, and their evident reasonableness.

PART V. BUDDHISM AND SCIENCE

325. Q. *Has Buddhism any right to be considered a scientific religion, or may it be classified as a "revealed" one?*

A. Most emphatically it is not a revealed religion. The Buddha did not so preach, nor is it so understood. On the contrary, he gave it out as the statement of eternal truths, which his predecessors had taught like himself.

326. Q. *Repeat again the name of the Sutta, in which the Buddha tells us not to believe in an alleged revelation without testing it by one's reason and experience?*

A. The Kālāma Sutta, of the Anguthara Nikāya.

327. Q. *Do Buddhists accept the theory that everything has been formed out of nothing by a Creator?*

A. The Buddha taught that two things are causeless, *viz.*, Ākāsha, and Nirvāna. Everything has come ont of Ākāsha, in obedience to a law of motion inherent in it, and, after a certain existence, passes away. Nothing ever came out of nothing. We do not believe in miracles; hence we deny creation, and cannot conceive of a creation of something out of nothing. Nothing organic is eternal. Everything is in a state of constant flux, and undergoing change and reformation, keeping up the continuity according to the law of evolution.

328. Q. *Is Buddhism opposed to education, and to the study of science?*

A. Quite the contrary: in the *Sigālowāda Sutta* in a discourse preached by the Buddha, He specified as one of the duties of a teacher that he should give his pupils "instruction in science and lore". The Buddha's higher teachings are for the enlightened, the wise, and the thoughtful.

329. Q. *Can you show any further endorsement of Buddhism by science?*

A. The Buddha's doctrine teaches that there were many progenitors of the human race; also that there is a principle of differentiation among men; certain individuals have a greater capacity for the rapid attainment of Wisdom and arrival at Nirvāna than others.

330. Q. *Any other?*

A. Buddhism supports the teaching of the indestructibility of force.

331. Q. *Should Buddhism be called a chart of science or a code of morals?*

A. Properly speaking, a pure moral philosophy, a system of ethics and transcendental metaphysics. It is so eminently practical that the Buddha kept silent when Malunka asked about the origin of things.

332. Q. *Why did he do that?*

A. Because he thought that our chief aim should be to see things as they exist around us and try to make them better, not to waste time in intellectual speculations.

333. Q. *What do Buddhists say is the reason for the occasional birth of very good and wise children of bad parents, and that of very bad ones of good parents?*

A. It is because of the respective Karmas of children and parents; each may have deserved that such unusual relationships should be formed in the present birth.

334. Q. *Is anything said about the body of the Buddha giving out a bright light?*

A. Yes, there was a divine radiance sent forth from within by the power of his holiness.

335. Q. *What is it called in Pāli?*

A. Buddharansi, the Buddha rays.

336. Q. *How many colours could be seen in it?*

A. Six, linked in pairs.

337. Q. *Their names?*

A. Nīla, Pita, Lohita, Avadata, Mangastā, Prabhasvra.

338. Q. *Did other persons emit such shining light?*

A. Yes, all Arhats did and, in fact, the light shines stronger and brighter in proportion to the spiritual development of the person.

339. Q. *Where do we see these colours represented?*

A. In all vihāras where there are painted images of the Buddha. They are also seen in the stripes of the Buddhist Flag, first made in Ceylon but now widely adopted throughout Buddhist countries.

340. Q. *In which discourse does the Buddha himself speak of this shining about him?*

A. In the *Mahā-Parinibbana Suttā*, Ānanda his favourite disciple, noticing the great splendour which came from his Master's body, the Buddha said that on two occasions this extraordinary shining occurs, (*a*) just after a Tathāgatā gains the supreme insight, and (*b*) on the night when he passes finally away.

341. Q. *Where do we read of this great brightness being emitted from the body of another Buddha?*

A. In the story of Sumedha and Dipānkāra Buddha, found in the *Nidānakathā* of the *Jātaka* book, or story of the reincarnations of the Bodhisattva Siddhārtha Gautama.

342. Q. *How is it described?*

A. As a halo of a fathom's depth.

343. Q. *What do the Hindus call it?*

A. *Tejas*; its extended radiance they call Prākāsha.

344. Q. *What do Europeans call it now?*

A. The human aura.

345. Q. *What great scientist has proved the existence of this aura by carefully conducted experiments?*

A. The Baron Von Reichenbach. His experiments are fully described in his *Researches*, published in 1844-5. Dr. Baraduc, of Paris, has, quite recently, photographed this light.

346. Q. *Is this bright aura a miracle or a natural phenomenon?*

A. Natural. It has been proved that not only all human beings but animals, trees, plants and even stones have it.

347. Q. *What peculiarity has it in the case of a Buddha or an Arhat?*

A. It is immensely brighter and more extended than in cases of other beings and objects. It is the evidence of their superior development in the power of *Iddhī*. The light has been seen coming from dāgobas in Ceylon where relics of the Buddha are said to be enshrined.

348. Q. *Do people of other religions besides Buddhism and Hindūism also believe in this light?*

A. Yes, in all pictures of Christian artists this light is represented as shining about the bodies of their holy personages. The same belief is found to have existed in other religions.

349. Q. *What historical incident supports the modern theory of hypnotic suggestion?*

A. That of Chullapanthaka, as told in the Pālī Commentary on the *Dhammapada*, etc.

350. Q. *Give me the facts.*

A. He was a bhikkhu who became an Arhat. On that very day the Buddha sent a messenger to call him. When the man reached the Vihāra, he saw three hundred bhikkhus in one group, each exactly like the others in every respect. On his asking which was Chullapanthaka, every one of the three hundred figures replied: "I am Chullapanthaka."

351. Q. *What did the messenger do?*

A. In his confusion he returned and reported to the Buddha.

352. Q. *What did the Buddha then tell him?*

A. To return to the vihāra and, if the same thing happened, to catch by the arm the *first* figure who said he was Chullapanthaka and lead him to him. The Buddha knew that the new Arhat would make this display of his acquired power to impress illusionary pictures of himself upon the messenger.

353. Q. *What is this power of illusion called in Pālī?*

A. *Manomaya Iddhī.*

354. Q. *Were the illusionary copies of the Arhat's person material? Were they composed of substance and could they have been felt and handled by the messenger?*

A. No; they were pictures impressed by his thought and trained will-power upon the messenger's mind.

355. Q. *To what would you compare them?*

A. To a man's reflection in a mirror, being exactly like him yet without solidity.

356. Q. *To make such an illusion on the messenger's mind, what was necessary?*

A. That Chullapanthaka should clearly conceive in his own mind his exact appearance, and then impress that, with as many duplicates or repetitions as he chose, upon the sensitive brain of the messenger.

357. Q. *What is this process now called?*

A. Hypnotic suggestion.

358. Q. *Could any third party have also seen these illusionary figures?*

A. That would depend on the will of the Arhat or hypnotiser.

359. Q. *What do you mean?*

A. Supposing that fifty or five hundred persons were there, instead of one, the Arhat could will that the illusion should be seen by all alike; or, if he chose, he could will that the messenger should be the only one to see them.

360. Q. *Is this branch of science well known in our day?*

A. Very well known; it is familiar to all students of mesmerism and hypnotism.

361. Q. *In what does our modern scientific belief support the theory of Karma, as taught in Buddhism?*

A. Modern scientists teach that every generation of men is heir to the consequences of the virtues and the vices of the preceding generation, not in the mass, as such, but in every individual case. Every one of us, according to Buddhism, gets a birth which represents the causes generated by him in an antecedent birth. This is the idea of Karma.

362. Q. *What say the Vāsettha Sutta about the causation in Nature?*

A. It says: "The world exists by cause; all things exist by cause, all beings are bound by cause."

363. Q. *Does Buddhism teach the unchangeableness of the visible universe; our earth, the sun, the moon, the stars, the mineral, vegetable, animal and human kingdoms?*

A. No. It teaches that all are constantly changing, and all must disappear in course of time.

364. Q. *Never to reappear?*

A. Not so: the principle of evolution, guided by Karma, individual and collective, will evolve another universe with its contents, as our universe was evolved out of the Ākāsha.

365. Q. *Does Buddhism admit that man has in his nature any latent powers for the production of phenomena commonly called "miracles"?*

A. Yes; but they are natural, not supernatural. They may be developed by a certain system which is laid down in our sacred books, the Visuddhi Mārga for instance.

366. Q. *What is this branch of science called?*

A. The Pāli name is Iddhi-vidhanānā.

367. Q. *How many kinds are there?*

A. Two: *Bāhira, i.e.,* one in which the phenomena-working power may be temporarily obtained by ascetic practices and also by resort to drugs, the recitation of *mantras* (charms), or other extraneous aids; and*Sasaniks*, that in which the power in question is acquired by interior self-development, and covers all and more than the phenomena of *Laukika Iddhī.*

368. Q. *What class of men enjoy these powers?*

A. They gradually develop in one which pursues a certain course of ascetic practice called *Dhyāna.*

369. Q. Can this Iddhi power be lost?[*]

A. The *Bāhira* can be lost, but the *Sasanika* never, when once acquired. *Lokottara* knowledge once obtained is never lost, and it is by this knowledge *only* that the absolute condition of Nirvāna is known by the Arhat. And this knowledge can be got by following the noble life of the Eightfold Path.

* Sumangala Sthavīra explains to me that those transcendent powers are permanently possessed only by one who has subdued all the passions (*Klesa*), in other words, an Arhat. The powers may be developed by a bad man and used for doing evil things, but their activity is but brief, the rebellious passions again dominate the sorcerer, and he becomes at last their victim.

370. Q. *Had Buddha the Lokottara Iddhī?*

A. Yes, in perfection.

371. Q. *And his disciples also had it?*

A. Yes, some but not all equally; the capacity for acquiring these occult powers varies with the individual.

372. Q. *Give examples?*

A. Of all the disciples of the Buddha, Mogallāna was possessed of the most extraordinary powers for making phenomena, while Ānanda could develop none during the twenty-five years in which he was the personal and intimate disciple of the Buddha himself. Later he did, as the Buddha had foretold he would.

373. Q. *Does a man acquire these powers suddenly or gradually?*

A. Normally, they gradually develop themselves as the disciple progressively gains control over his lower nature in a series of births.[*]

* When the powers suddenly show themselves, the inference is that the individual had developed himself in the next anterior birth. We do not believe in eccentric breaks in natural law.

374. Q. *Does Buddhism pretend that the miracle of raising those who are dead is possible?*

A. No. The Buddha teaches the contrary, in that beautiful story of Kisā Gotami and the mustard-seed. But when a person only seems to be dead but is not actually so, resuscitation is possible.

375. Q. *Give me an idea of these successive stages of the Lokottara development in Iddhī?*

A. There are six degrees attainable by Arhats; what is higher than them is to be reached only by a Buddha.

376. Q. *Describe the six stages or degrees?*

A. We may divide them into two groups, of three each. The first to include (1) Progressive retrospection, *viz.*, a gradually acquired power to look backward in time towards the origin of things; (2) Progressive foresight, or power of prophecy; (3) Gradual extinction of desires and attachments to material things.

377. Q. *What would the second group include?*

A. The same faculties, but inimitably developed. Thus, the full Arhat possesses perfect retrospection, perfect foresight, and has absolutely extinguished the last trace of desire and selfish attractions.

378. Q. *What are the four means for obtaining Iddhī?*

A. The will, its exertion, mental development, and discrimination between right and wrong.

379. Q. *Our Scriptures relate hundreds of instances of phenomena produced by Arhats: what did you say was the name of this faculty or power?*

A. *Iddhī vidha.* One possessing this can, by manipulating the forces of Nature, produce any wonderful phenomenon, *i.e.*, make any scientific experiment he chooses.

380. Q. *Did the Buddha encourage displays of phenomena?*

A. No; he expressly discouraged them as tending to create confusion in the minds of those who were not acquainted with the principles involved. They also tempt their possessors to show them merely to gratify idle curiosity and their own vanity. Moreover, similar phenomena can be shown by magicians and sorcerers learned in the *Laukika*, or the baser form of *Iddhī* science. All false pretensions to supernatural attainment by monks are among the unpardonable sins (*Tevijja Sutta*).

381. Q. *You spoke of a "deva" having appeared to the Prince Siddhārtha under a variety of forms; what do Buddhists believe respecting races of elemental invisible beings having relations with mankind?*

A. They believe that there are such beings who inhabit worlds or spheres of their own. The Buddhist doctrine is that, by interior self-development and conquest over his baser nature, the Arhat becomes superior to even the most formidable of the devas, and may subject and control the lower orders.

382. Q. *How many kinds of devas are there?*

A. Three: *Kāmāvacharā* (those who are still under the domination of the passions); *Rūpāvacharā* (a higher class, which still retain an individual form): *Arāpāvacharā* (the highest in degree of purification, who are devoid of material forms).

383. Q. *Should we fear any of them?*

A. He who is pure and compassionate in heart and of a courageous mind need fear nothing: no man, god, *brahmarakkhas*, demon or deva, can injure him, but some have power to torment the impure, as well as those who invite their approach.

APPENDIX

The following text of the fourteen items of belief which have been accepted as fundamental principles in both the Southern and Northern sections of Buddhism, by authoritative committees to whom they were submitted by me personally, have so much historical importance that they are added to the present edition of THE BUDDHIST CATECHISM as an Appendix. It has very recently been reported to me by H. E. Prince Ouchtomsky, the learned Russian Orientalist, that having had the document translated to them, the Chief Lamas of the great Mongolian Buddhist monasteries declared to him that they accept every one of the propositions as drafted, with the one exception that the date of the Buddha is by them believed to have been some thousands of years earlier than the one given by me. This surprising fact had not hitherto come to my knowledge. Can it be that the Mongolian Sangha confuse the real epoch of Sākya Muni with that of his alleged next predecessor? Be this as it may, it is a most encouraging fact that the whole Buddhistic world may now be said to have united to the extent at least of these Fourteen Propositions.

H. S. O.

FUNDAMENTAL BUDDHISTIC BELIEFS

I Buddhists are taught to show the same tolerance, forbearance, and brotherly love to all men, without distinction; and an unswerving kindness towards the members of the animal kingdom.

II The universe was evolved, not created; and its functions according to law, not according to the caprice of any God.

III The truths upon which Buddhism is founded are natural. They have, we believe, been taught in successive kalpas, or world-periods, by certain illuminated beings called BUDDHAS, the name BUDDHA meaning "Enlightened".

IV The fourth Teacher in the present kalpa was Sākya Muni, or Gautama Buddha, who was born in a Royal family in India about 2,500 years ago. He is an historical personage and his name was Siddhārtha Gautama.

V Sākya Muni taught that ignorance produces desire, unsatisfied desire is the cause of rebirth, and rebirth, the cause of sorrow. To get rid of sorrow, therefore, it is necessary to escape rebirth; to escape rebirth, it is necessary to extinguish desire; and to extinguish desire, it is necessary to destroy ignorance.

VI Ignorance fosters the belief that rebirth is a necessary thing. When ignorance is destroyed the worthlessness of every such rebirth, considered as an end in itself, is perceived, as well as the paramount need of adopting a course of life by which the necessity for such repeated rebirths can be abolished. Ignorance also begets the illusive and illogical idea that there is only one existence for man, and the other illusion that this one life is followed by states of unchangeable pleasure or torment.

VII The dispersion of all this ignorance can be attained by the persevering practice of an all-embracing altruism in conduct, development of intelligence, wisdom in thought, and destruction of desire for the lower personal pleasures.

VIII The desire to live being the cause of rebirth, when that is extinguished rebirths cease and the perfected individual attains by meditation that highest state of peace called *Nirvāna*.

IX Sākya Muni taught that ignorance can be dispelled and sorrow removed by the knowledge of the four Noble Truths, *viz.*:

1. The miseries of existence;

2. The cause productive of misery, which is the desire ever renewed of satisfying oneself without being able ever to secure that end;

3. The destruction of that desire, or the estranging of oneself from it;

4. The means of obtaining this destruction of desire. The means which he pointed out is called the Noble Eightfold Path, *viz.*: Right Belief; Right Thought; Right Speech; Right Action; Right Means of Livelihood; Right Exertion; Right Remembrance; Right Meditation.

X Right Meditation leads to spiritual enlightenment, or the development of that Buddha-like faculty which is latent in every man.

XI The essence of Buddhism, as summed up by the Tathāgathā (Buddha) himself, as:

To cease from all sin,

To get virtue,

To purify the heart.

XII The universe is subject to a natural causation known as "Karma". The merits and demerits of a being in past existences determine his condition in the present one. Each man, therefore, has prepared the causes of the effects which he now experiences.

XIII The obstacles to the attainment of good karma may be removed by the observance of the following precepts, which are embraced in the moral code of Buddhism, *viz.*: (1) Kill not; (2) Steal not; (3) Indulge in no forbidden sexual pleasure; (4) Lie not; (5) Take no intoxication or stupefying drug or liquor. Five other precepts which need not be here enumerated should be observed by those who would attain, more quickly than the average layman, the release from misery and rebirth.

XIV Buddhism discourages superstitious credulity. Gautama Buddha taught it to be the duty of a parent to have his child educated in science and literature. He also taught that no one should believe what is spoken by any sage, written in any book, or affirmed by tradition, unless it accord with reason.

Drafted as a common platform upon which all Buddhists can agree.

H. S. OLCOTT, P.T.S.

Respectfully submitted for the approval of the High Priests of the nations which we severally represent, in the Buddhist Conference held at Adyar, Madras, on the 8th, 9th, 10th, 11th, and 12th of January, 1891 (A.B. 2434).

Japan . . . . . (Kozen Gunaratana

(Chiezo Tokuzawa

Burmah . . . . . U. Hmoay Tha Aung

Ceylon . . . . . Dhammapala Hevavitarana.

The Maghs of Chittagong . . . Krshna Chandra Chowdry, by his appointed Proxy, Maung Tha Dwe.

BURMAH

Approved on behalf of the Buddhists of Burmah, this 3rd day of February, 1891 (A. B. 2434):

Tha-tha-na-baing Saydawgyi; Aung Myi Shwebōn Sayadaw; Me-ga-waddy Sayadaw; Hmat-Khaya Sayadaw; Hti-lin Sayadaw; Myadaung Sayadaw; Hla-Htwe Sayadaw; and sixteen others.

CEYLON

Approved on behalf of the Buddhists of Ceylon this 25th day of February, 1891 (A.B. 2434); Mahannwara upawsatha puspārāma vihārādhipati Hippola Dhamma Rakkhita Sobhitābhidhāna Mahā Nāyaka Sthavirayan wahanse wamha.

(Hippola Dhamma Rakkhita Sabhitābhidhana, High Priest of the Malwatta Vihare at Kandy).

(Sd.) HIPPOLA.

Mahanuwara Asgiri vihārādhipati Yatawattē Chandajottyābhidhana Mahā Nāyaka Sthavirayan wahanse wamha—(Yatawattē Chandajottyābhidhana, High Priest of Asgiri Tihare at Kandy).

(Sd.) YATAWATTE

Hikkaduwe Srī Sumangala Sripādasthāne saha Kolamba palate pradhāna Nāyaka Sthavirayo (Hikkaduwe Srī Sumangala, High Priest of Adam's Peak and the District of Colombo).

(Sd.) H. SUMANGALA

Maligawe Prāchina Pustakālāyadhyakshaka Suriyagoda Sonuttara Sthavirayo (Suriyagoda Sonuttara, Librarian of the Oriental Library at the Temple of the Tooth Relic at Kandy).

(Sd.) S. SONUTTARA

Sugata Sāsanadhaja Vinayā chāriya Dhammalankārābhidhāna Nāyaka Sthavira.

(Sd.) W. DHAMMALANKARA

Pawara neruttika chariya Mahā Vibhavi Subhuti of Waskaduwa.

(Sd.) W. SUBHUTI

JAPAN

Accepted as included within the body of Northern Buddhism.

Shaku Genyu   (Shingon   Shu)
Fukuda Nichiyo   (Nichiren   ")
Sanada Seyko   (Zen   ")
Ito Quan Shyu   ("   ")
Takehana Hakuyo   (Jodo   ")
Kono Rioshin   (Ji-Shu   ")
Kiro Ki-ko   (Jodo Seizan ")
Harutani Shinsho (Tendai   ")
Manabe Shun-myo   (Shingon   ")

CHITTAGONG

Accepted for the Buddhists of Chittagong.

Nagawa Parvata Vihāarādhipati
Guna Megu Wini-Lankara,
Harbing, Chittagong, Bengal.

BIBLIOGRAPHY

The Buddhist Catechism has been compiled from personal studies in Ceylon, and in part from the following works:

Vinaya Texts . . . . Davids and Oldenberg.
Buddhist Literature in China . . . . . . Beal.
Catena of Buddhist Scriptures . . . . . Do.
Buddhaghosa's Parables . . . . Rogers.
Buddhist Birth Stories . . . . Fausboll and Davids.
Legend of Gautama . . . . Bigandet.
Chinese Buddhism . . . . Edkins.
Kalpa Sutra and Nava Patva . . . . . . Stevenson.
Buddha and Early Buddhism . . . . . . Lillie.
Sutta Nipāta . . . . Sir Coomara Swami.
Nāgananda . . . . Broyd.

Kusa Jataka . . . . Steele.
Buddhism . . . . Rhys-Davids.
Dhammapada . . . . Fausboll and Max Müller.
Romantic History of Buddha . . . . Beal.
Udānavarga . . . . Rockhill.
Twelve Japanese Buddhist Sects . . . . . B. Nanjio.
The Gospel of Buddha . . . . Paul Carus.
The Dharma . . . . Do.
Ancient India . . . . R. C. Dutt.
The "Sacred Books of the East" Series . Max Müller's Edition.
Encyclopædia Britannica

THE END

BOOK TWO

THE LIFE OF BUDDHA AND ITS LESSONS

The thoughtful student, in scanning the religious history of the race, has one fact continually forced upon his notice, *viz.*, that there is an invariable tendency to deify whomsoever shows himself superior to the weakness of our common humanity. Look where we will, we find the saint-like man exalted into a divine personage and worshipped for a god. Though perhaps misunderstood, reviled and even persecuted while living, the apotheosis is almost sure to come after death: and the victim of yesterday's mob, raised to the state of an Intercessor in Heaven, is besought with prayer and tears, and placatory penances, to mediate with God for the pardon of human sin. This is a mean and vile trait of human nature, the proof of ignorance, selfishness, brutal cowardice, and a superstitious materialism. It shows the base instinct to put down and destroy whatever or whoever makes men feel their own imperfections; with the alternative of ignoring and denying these very imperfections by turning into gods men who have merely spiritualised their natures, so that it may be supposed that they were heavenly incarnations and not mortal like other men.

This process of euhemerisation, as it is called, or the making of men into gods and gods into men, sometimes, though more rarely, begins during the life of the hero, but usually after death. The true history of his life is gradually amplified and decorated with fanciful incidents, to fit it to the new character which has been posthumously given him. Omens and portents are now made to attend his earthly avat□āra: his precocity is described as superhuman: as a babe or lisping child he silences the wisest logicians by his divine knowledge: miracles he produces as other boys do soap-bubbles: the terrible energies of nature are his playthings: the gods, angels, and demons are his habitual attendants: the sun, moon, and all the starry host wheel around his cradle in joyful measures, and the earth thrills with joy at having borne such a prodigy: and at his last hour of mortal life the whole universe shakes with conflicting emotions.

Why need I use the few moments at my disposal to marshal before you the various personages of whom these fables have been written? Let it suffice to recall the interesting fact to your notice, and invite you to compare the respective biographies of the Brāhman□ical Kr□s□hn□a, the Persian Zoroaster, the Egyptian Hermes, the Indian Gaut□ama, and the canonical, especially the apocryphal, Jesus. Taking Kr□s□hn□a or Zoroaster, as you please, as the most ancient, and coming down the chronological line of descent, you will find them all made after the same pattern. The real personage is all covered up and concealed under the embroidered veils of the romancer and the enthusiastic historiographer. What is surprising to me is that this tendency to exaggeration and hyperbole is not more commonly allowed for by those who in our days attempt to discuss and compare religions. We are constantly and painfully reminded that the prejudice of inimical critics, on the one hand, and the furious bigotry of devotees, on the other, blind men to fact and probability, and lead to gross injustice. Let me take as an example the mythical biographies of Jesus. At the time when the Council of Nicea was convened for settling the quarrels of certain bishops, and for the purpose of examining into the canonicity of the three hundred more or less apocryphal gospels that were being read in the Christian churches as inspired writings, the history of the life of Christ had reached the height of absurd myth. We may see some specimens in the extant books of the apocryphal New Testament, but most of them are now lost. What have been retained in the present Canon may doubtless be regarded as the least objectionable. And yet we must not hastily adopt even this conclusion, for you know that Sabina, Bishop of Heracha, himself speaking of the Council of Nicea, affirms that "except Constantine and Sabinus, Bishop of Pamphilus, these bishops were a set of illiterate, simple creatures that understood nothing"; which is as though he had said they were a pack of fools. And Pappus, in his *Synodicon* to that Council of Nicea, lets us into the secret that the Canon was not decided by a careful comparison of several gospels before them, but by a *lottery*. Having, he tells us, "promiscuously put all the books that were referred to the Council for determination under a Communion table in a church, they (the bishops) besought the Lord that the inspired writings might get up on the table, while the spurious writings remained underneath, and *it happened accordingly*".

But letting all this pass and looking only to what is contained in the present Canon, we see the same tendency to compel all nature to attest the divinity of the writer's hero. At the nativity a star leaves its orbit and leads the Persian astrologers to the divine child, and angels come and converse with shepherds, and a whole train of like celestial phenomena occurs at various stages of his earthly career, which closes amid earthquakes, a pall of darkness over the whole scene, a supernatural war of the elements, the opening of graves and the walking about of their tenants, and other appalling wonders. Now, if the candid Bud☐d☐hist concedes that the real history of Gaut☐ama is embellished by like absurd exaggerations, and if we can find their duplicates in the biographies of Zoroaster, Shankarāchārya and other real personages of antiquity, have we not the right to conclude that the true history of the Founder of Christianity, if at this late date it were possible to write it, would be very different from the narratives that pass current? We must not forget that Jerusalem was at that time a Roman dependency, just as Ceylon is now a British, and that the silence of contemporary Roman historians about any such violent disturbances of the equilibrium of nature is deeply significant.

I have cited this example for the sole and simple purpose of bringing home to the non-Bud☐d☐histic portion of my present audience the conviction that, in considering the life of Sākya Muni and the lessons it teaches, they must not make his followers of to-day responsible for any extravagant exuberances of past biographers. The doctrine of Bud☐d☐ha and its effects are to be judged quite apart from the man, just as the doctrine ascribed to Jesus and its effects are to be considered quite irrespectively of his personal history. And—as I hope I have shown—the actual doings and sayings of every founder of a Faith or a school of philosophy must be sought for under a heap of tinsel and rubbish contributed by successive generations of followers.

Approaching the question of the hour in this spirit of precaution, what do we find are the probabilities respecting the life of Sākya Muni? Who was he? When did he live? How did he live? What did he teach? A most careful comparison of authorities and analysis of evidence establishes, I think, the following data:

1. He was the son of a king.

2. He lived between six and seven centuries before Christ.

3. He resigned his royal state and went to live in the jungle, and among the lowest and most unhappy classes, so as to learn the secret of human pain and misery by personal experience: tested every known austerity of the Hind☐ū ascetics and excelled them all in his power of endurance: sounded every depth of woe in search of the means to alleviate it: and at last came out victorious, and showed the world the way to salvation.

4. What he taught may be summed up in a few words, as the perfume of many roses may be distilled into a few drops of *attar*: Everything in

the world of Matter is unreal; the only reality is in the world of Spirit. Emancipate yourselves from the tyranny of the former; strive to attain the latter. The Rev. Samuel Beal, in his *Catena of Bud□d□hist Scriptures from the Chinese* puts it differently. "The idea underlying the Buddhist religious system is," he says, "simply this: 'all is vanity'. Earth is a show, and Heaven is a vain reward." Primitive Bud□d□hism was engrossed, absorbed, by one thought—the vanity of finite existence, the priceless value of the one condition of Eternal Rest.

If I have the temerity to prefer my own definition of the spirit of Bud□d□ha's doctrine, it is because I think that all the misconceptions of it have arisen from a failure to understand his idea of what is real and what is unreal, what worth longing and striving for and what not. From this misconception have come all the unfounded charges that Bud□d□hism is an "atheistical," that is to say, a grossly materialistic, a nihilistic, a negative, a vice-breeding religion. Bud□d□hism denies the existence of a personal God—true: therefore—well, therefore, and notwithstanding all this, its teaching is neither what may be called properly atheistical, nihilistic, negative, nor provocative of vice. I will try to make my meaning clear, and the advancement of modern scientific research helps in this direction. Science divides the universe for us into two elements—matter and force; accounting for their phenomena by their combinations, and making both eternal and obedient to eternal and immutable law. The speculations of men of science have carried them to the outermost verge of the physical universe. Behind them lie not only a thousand brilliant triumphs by which a part of Nature's secrets have been wrung from her, but also more thousands of failures to fathom her deep mysteries. They have proved thought material, since it is the evolution of the gray tissue of the brain, and a recent German experimentalist, Professor Dr. Jäger, claims to have proved that man's soul is "a volatile odoriferous principle, capable of solution in glycerine". Psychogen is the name he gives to it, and his experiments show that it is present not merely in the body as a whole, but in every individual cell, in the ovum, and even in the ultimate elements of protoplasm. I need hardly say to so intelligent an audience as this, that these highly interesting experiments of Dr. Jäger are corroborated by many facts, both physiological and psychological, that have been always noticed among all nations; facts which are woven into popular proverbs, legends, folk-lore fables, mythologies and theologies, the world over. Now, if thought is matter and soul is matter, then Bud□d□ha, in recognising the impermanence of sensual enjoyment or experience of any kind, and the instability of every material form, the human soul included, uttered a profound and scientific truth, And since the very idea of gratification or suffering is inseparable from that of material being— absolute SPIRIT alone being regarded by common consent as perfect, changeless and Eternal—therefore, in teaching the doctrine that conquest of the material self, with all its lusts, desires, loves, hopes, ambitions and hates, frees one from pain, and leads to Nirvān□a, the state of Perfect Rest, he preached the rest of an untinged, untainted existence in the Spirit. Though the soul be composed of the finest conceivable substance, yet if substance at all—as Dr. Jäger seems able to prove, and ages of human intercourse with the weird phantoms of the shadow world imply—it must in time perish. What remains is that changeless part of man, which most philosophers call Spirit, and Nirvān□a is its necessary condition of existence. The only dispute between Bud□d□hist authorities is whether this Nirvān□ic existence is attended with individual consciousness, or whether the individual is merged in the whole, as the extinguished flame is lost in the air. But there are those who say that the flame has not been annihilated by the blowing out. It has only passed out of the visible world of matter into the invisible world of Spirit, where it still exists and will ever exist, as a bright reality. Such thinkers can understand Bud□d□ha's doctrine and, while agreeing with him that soul is not immortal, would spurn the charge of materialistic nihilism, if brought against either that sublime teacher or themselves.

The history of Sākya Muni's life is the strongest bulwark of his religion. As long as the human heart is capable of being touched by tales of heroic self-sacrifice, accompanied by purity and celestial benevolence of motive, it will cherish his memory. Why should I go into the particulars of that noble life? You will remember that he was the son of the king of Kapilavast□u—a mighty sovereign whose opulence enabled him to give the heir of his house every luxury that a voluptuous imagination could desire: and that the future Bud□d□ha was not allowed even to know, much less observe, the miseries of ordinary existence. How beautifully Edwin Arnold has painted for us in *The Light of Asia* the luxury and languor of that Indian Court, "where love was gaoler and delights its bars". We are told that:

The king commanded that within those walls

No mention should be made of age or death

Sorrow or pain, or sickness ...

And every dawn the dying rose was plucked,

The dead leaves hid, all evil sights removed:

For said the king, "If he shall pass his youth
Far from such things as move to wistfulness
And brooding on the empty eggs of thought,
The shadow of this fate, too vast for man,
May fade, belike, and I shall see him grow
To that great stature of fair sovereignty,
When he shall rule all lands—if he *will rule*—
The king of kings and glory of his time."

You know how vain were all the precautions taken by the father to prevent the fulfilment of the prophecy that his beloved son would be the coming Bud□d□ha. Though all suggestions of death were banished from the royal palace, though the city was bedecked with flowers and gay flags, and every painful object removed from sight when the young Prince Sid□d□ārtha visited it, yet the decrees of destiny were not to be baffled, the "voices of the spirits," the "wandering winds" and the d□evas, whispered the truth of human sorrows into his listening ear, and when the appointed hour arrived, the Sud□d□ha D□evas threw the spell of slumber over the household, steeped in profound lethargy the sentinels (as we are told was done by an angel to the gaolers of Peter's prison), rolled back the triple gates of bronze, strewed the sweet moghra-flowers thickly beneath his horse's feet to muffle every sound, and he was free. Free? Yes—to resign every earthly comfort, every sensuous enjoyment, the sweets of royal power, the homage of a Court, the delights of domestic life: gems, the glitter of gold: rich stuffs, rich food, soft beds: the songs of trained musicians, and of birds kept prisoners in gay cages, the murmur of perfumed waters plashing in marble basins, the delicious shade of trees in gardens where art had contrived to make nature even lovelier than herself. He leaps from his saddle when at a safe distance from the palace, flings the jewelled rein to his faithful groom, Channa, cuts off his flowing locks, gives his rich costume to a hunter in exchange for his own, plunges into the jungle, and is free:

To tread its paths with patient, stainless feet,
Making its dusty bed, its loneliest wastes
My dwelling, and its meanest things my mates:
Clad in no prouder garb than outcasts wear,
Fed with no meals save what the charitable
Give of their will, sheltered by no more pomp,
Than the dim cave lends or the jungle-bush.

This will I do because the woeful cry
Of life and all flesh living cometh up
Into my ears, and all my soul is full
Of pity for the sickness of this world:
Which I will heal, if healing may be found
By uttermost renouncing and strong strife.

Thus masterfully does Sir Edwin Arnold depict the sentiment which provoked this Great Renunciator. The testimony of thousands of millions who, during the last twenty-five centuries, have professed the Bud☐d☐histic religion, proves that the secret of human misery was at last solved by this divine self-sacrifice, and the true path to Nirvān☐a opened.

The joy that he brought to the hearts of others, Bud☐d☐ha first tasted himself. He found that the pleasures of the eye, the ear, the taste, touch and smell are fleeting and deceptive: he who gives value to them brings only disappointment and bitter sorrow upon himself. The social differences between men he found were equally arbitrary and illusive; caste bred hatred and selfishness; riches strife, envy and malice. So in founding his Faith he laid the bottom of its foundation-stones upon all this worldly dirt, and its dome in the clear serene of the world of Spirit. He who can mount to a clear conception of Nirvān☐a will find his thought far away above the common joys and sorrows of petty men. As to one who ascends to the top of Chimborazo or the Himālayan crags, and sees men on the earth's surface crawling to and fro like ants, so equally small do bigots and sectarians appear to him. The mountain climber has under his feet the very clouds from whose sun-painted shapes the poet has figured to himself the golden streets and glittering domes of the materialistic Heaven of a personal God. Below him are all the various objects out of which the world's pantheons have been manufactured: around, above—Immensity. And so also, far down the ascending plane of thought that leads from the earth towards the Infinite, the philosophic Bud☐d☐hist describes, at different plateaux, the heavens and hells, the gods and demons, of the materialistic creed-builders.

What are the lessons to be derived from the life and teachings of this heroic prince of Kapilavast☐u? Lessons of gratitude and benevolence. Lessons of tolerance for the clashing opinions of men who live, move and have their being, think and aspire, only in the material world. The lesson of a common tie of brotherhood among all men. Lessons of manly self-reliance, of equanimity in breasting whatsoever of good or ill may happen. Lessons of the meanness of the rewards, the pettiness of the misfortunes of a shifting world of illusions. Lessons of the necessity for avoiding every species of evil thought and word, and for doing, speaking and thinking everything that is good, and for the bringing of the mind into subjection so that these may be accomplished without selfish motive or vanity. Lessons of self-purification and communion, by which the illusiveness of externals and the value of internals are understood.

Well might St. Hilaire burst into the panegyric that Bud☐d☐ha "is the perfect model of all the virtues he preaches ... his life has not a stain upon it". Well might the sober critic Max Müller pronounce his moral code "one of the most perfect which the world has ever known". No wonder that in contemplating that gentle life Edwin Arnold should have found his personality "the highest, gentlest, holiest and most beneficent ... in the history of thought," and been moved to write his splendid verses. It is twenty-five hundred years since humanity put forth such a flower: who knows when it did before?

Gaut☐ama Bud☐d☐ha, Sākya Muni, has ennobled the whole human race. His fame is our common inheritance. His Law is the law of Justice, providing for every good thought, word and deed its fair reward, for every evil one its proper punishment. His law is in harmony with the voices of Nature, and the evident equilibrium of the universe. It yields nothing to importunities or threats, can be neither coaxed nor bribed by offerings to abate or alter one jot or tittle of its inexorable course. Am I told that Bud☐d☐hist laymen display vanity in their worship and ostentation in their almsgiving; that they are fostering sects as bitterly as Hind☐ūs? So much the worse for the laymen: there is the example of Bud☐d☐ha and his Law. Am I told that Bud☐d☐hist priests are ignorant, idle fosterers of superstitions grafted on their religion by foreign kings? So much the worse for the priests: the life of their Divine Master shames them and shows their unworthiness to wear his yellow robe or carry his beggar's bowl. There is the Law—immutable—menacing; it will find them out and punish.

And what shall we say to those of another caste of character—the humble-minded, charitable, tolerant, religiously aspiring hearts among the laity, and the unselfish, pure and learned of the priests who know the Precepts and keep them? The Law will find them out also; and when the book of each life is written up and the balance struck, every good thought or deed will be found entered in its proper place. Not one blessing that ever followed them from grateful lips throughout their earthly pilgrimage will be found to have been lost; but each will help to ease their way as they move from stage to stage of Being

Unto Nirvān□a where the Silence Lives.

THE END

BOOK THREE

THE GOLDEN RULES OF BUDDHISM*

*Compiled from the same sources as Buddhist Catechism.

PREFACE

THE too prevalent ignorance among even adult Sinhalese Buddhists of the ethical code of their religion heads me to issue this little compilation. Similar moral precepts exist by hundreds in the Buddhist Scriptures; where, also, all the present quotations will be found in the places indicated. They should be committed to memory and practised by parents and taught to their children, especially when the latter are being educated under anti-Buddhistic influences.

Orientalists and other impartial persons admit that no religion in the world contains a more sublime system of moral rules than Buddhism, but if we wish this to become known to Buddhist children, we adult Buddhists must take the task upon ourselves. Many a Buddhist boy has beet "converted " to Christianity, or otherwise brought to despise his ancestral religion, from ignorance of its merits.

- H. S. O.

ADYAR, MADRAS
17th November, 1887

Merits and Demerits

LET him [the householder] not destroy, or cause to be destroyed, any life at all, or sanction the acts of those who do so.* Let him refrain from even hurting any creature,** both those that are strong, and those that tremble in the world.

(Dhammika Sutta, v. 19)

* One who buys butcher's meat or poultry violates this gatha. For, by paying the butcher for meat he has killed, the buyer shares his sin by "sanctioning" his act.

** An inaccurate expression, adopted from Christian writers. A "creature" is something created (by God), but Buddhists regard all living organisms as evolved by the process of natural law.

****

A disciple then knowing [the law] should refrain from stealing anything at any place; should not cause another to steal anything, should not consent to the acts of those who steal anything, should avoid every kind of theft.

(Dhammika Sutta, v. 20)

****

A wise man should avoid unchastity as if it were a burning pit of live coals. One who is not able to live in a state of celibacy should not commit adultery.*

(Dhammika Sutta, v. 21)

* The history of all monastic establishments shows that there are persons temperamentally unfit for celibate life, and whose lapses bring great scandal upon their orders. The Sangha has not escaped this misery, offenders having been noted even in our Lord's own time. Yet the general blamelessness of Buddhist monks has been acknowledged even by clerical opponents. A true regard to the honour of the Sangha should prompt senior priests to insist upon the relinquishment of the robe by such as are not sexually self-masterful. "It is better to marry than burn", says St. Paul.

****

Four things does a reckless man obtain who covets his neighbour's wife - a bad reputation; an uncomfortable bed; thirdly, punishment; lastly, future torment.

(Dhammapada, v. 309)

****

Of all the lusts and desires, there is none so powerful as sexual inclination. This is so strong that there is no other worth speaking of beyond it. . . . Lust and desire, in respect of a man, are like a person who takes a lighted torch and runs with it against the wind.

(Sutra of the 42 Sections, Beal's Catena, p. 198)

****

When one is come to a royal assembly [i.e., any official inquiry], he should not tell lies to anyone, or cause any to tell lies, or consent to the acts of those who tell lies; he should avoid every kind of untruth.

(Dhammika Sutta, v. 22)

****

The householder who delights in the Law should not indulge in intoxicating drinks [or stupefying drugs], should not cause others to drink, should not sanction the acts of those who drink,* knowing that it results in insanity.

(Dhammika Sutta, v. 23)

* Then no Buddhist can without grievous sin become an arrack renter, or seller, or drinker.

[4]

****

He who destroys life, who speaks untruth, who takes in this world what is not given him, who takes another man's wife, and the man who gives himself up to drinking intoxicating liquors: he, even in this world, digs up his own root.

(Dhammapada, vv. 246, 247)

****

The ignorant commit sins in consequence of drunkenness, and also make others drink. You should avoid this: it is the cause of demerit, insanity and ignorance - though it be pleasing to the ignorant.

(Dhammika Sutta, v. 24)

****

The fields are damaged by weeds, mankind by passion; therefore a gift bestowed on the passionless brings great reward.

(Dhammapada, v. 356)

****

The virtuous man is happy in this world, and he is happy in the next; he is happy in both.

He is happy when he thinks of the good he has done; he is still more happy when going in the good path.

(Dhammapada, v. 18)

****

What ought to be done is neglected, what ought not to be done is done; the sins of unruly, thoughtless people are always increasing.

(Dhammapada, v. 292)

****

Let each man make himself as he teaches others to be; he who is well subdued may subdue [others]; one's own self is difficult to subdue.

(Dhammapada, v. 159)

****

Whoever, being asked for what is good, teaches what is not good, [and] advises [another] concealing something from him, know him to be a Vasala.*

(Vasala Sutta, v. 11)

* A slave.

Passions

Hatred is never quenched by hatred: hatred ceases by [showing] love; this is an old rule.

(Dhammapada, v. 5)

****

Let a man overcome anger by love, evil by good, the greedy by liberality, the liar by truth.

(Dhammapada, v. 223)

****

Do not speak harshly to anybody; those who are spoken to, will answer thee in the same way.

(Dhammapada, v. 133)

****

Cut down the whole forest of lust, not one tree. When thou hast cut down every tree and every shrub, then thou wilt be free.

(Dhammapada, v. 283)

****

Not nakedness, not matted hair, not dirt, not fasting, not lying on the earth, not rubbing with dust, not sitting motionless, can purify a mortal who has not overcome desires.

(Dhammapada, v. 141)

****

If a man becomes fat and a great eater, if he is sleepy and rolls himself about, that fool, like a hog fed on slops, is born again and again.

(Dhammapada, v. 325)

****

The avaricious go not to the world of the gods [devas], for the fool commends not charity.

(Udanavarga, x. v. 2)

****

He who holds back rising anger like a rolling chariot, him I call a real driver; other people are but holders of the reins.

(Dhammapada, v. 222)

****

A wicked man who reproaches a virtuous one, is like one who looks up and spits at the sky; the spittle soils not the sky, but comes back and defiles his own person. So again, he is like one who flings dirt at another when wind is contrary; the dirt does but return on him who threw it. The virtuous man cannot be hurt, the misery that the other would inflict comes back on himself.

(Sutra of the 42 Sections, Beal's Catena, p. 193)

****

The fool who is angered and who thinks to triumph by using abusive language, is always vanquished by him whose words are patient.

(Udanavarga, xx, v. 14)

****

The fault of others is easily perceived, but that of oneself is difficult to perceive; the faults of others one lays open as much as possible, but one's own fault one hides, as a cheat hides the bad die from the gambler.

If a man looks after the faults of others, and is always inclined to detract, his own weakness will grow.

(Dhammapada, vv. 252, 253)

****

What is called "Name" or "Tribe", in the world, arises from usage only. It is adopted here and there by common consent. It comes from long and uninterrupted usage, and from the false belief of the ignorant.

(Vasettha Sutta, vv. 55, 56)

****

Whatever man is proud of his caste, is proud of his wealth, is proud of his family [and] despises his relations, that [man] is a cause of suffering loss.

(Parabhava Sutta, v. 14)

****

Anger, drunkenness, obstinacy, bigotry, deception, envy, self-praise, disparaging others, highmindedness [conceit?], evil communications, these constitute uncleanness; not verily the eating of flesh.

Neither abstinence from fish or flesh, nor going naked, nor the shaving of the head, nor matted hair, nor dirt, etc., etc., etc., will cleanse a man not free from delusions.*

(Amagandha Sutta, vv. 7,11)

* The meaning of the Teacher is here so obvious that I cannot understand how this Sutta could have ever been cited as authority for

85

buying and eating butcher's meat. Nothing herein lessens the force of the positive instruction in the Dhammika Sutta (v. ante) to abstain both from destroying, causing to be destroyed, or sanctioning the acts of those who destroy the life of any being. I know a large and increasing number of Sinhalese indulge in meat-eating, and quiet their consciences by quoting the above gathas; and I have listened with amusement to the sophistical argument that the sin of the killing is with the butcher and not with his sanctioning and abetting customer. Still, I must hold to my opinion until the problematical future time when black shall be proved white.

Associates and Friends

He who walks in the company of fools, suffers a long way; company with fools, as with an enemy, is always painful; company with the wise is pleasure, like meeting with kinsfolk. (Dhammapada, v. 207)

****

Therefore one ought to follow the wise, the intelligent, the learned, the much-enduring, the dutiful; one ought to follow a good and wise man as the moon follows the path of the stars. (Dhammapada, v. 208) .

****

Good people shine from afar like the snowy mountains [the Himalayas]; bad people are not seen, like arrows shot at night.
(Dhammapada, v. 304)

****

If a traveler does not meet with one who is his better, or equal, let him firmly keep his solitary journey; there is no companionship with a fool.
(Dhammapada, v. 61)

****

If any intelligent person be associated for even one moment with a wise man, he will soon perceive the fact.
(Dhammapada, v. 65)

PART II

Parents, Teachers and Children

Parents should:
1. Restrain their children from vice.
2. Train them in virtue.
3. Have them taught arts and sciences.

4. Provide them with suitable wives or husbands.
5. Give them an inheritance.

The child should say:
1. I will support them who supported me.
2. I will perform family duties incumbent upon them.
3. I will guard their property.
4. I will make myself worthy to be their heir.
5. When they are gone I will honour their memory.
(Sigalovada Sutta)

****

Happy in this world is he who honours his father, so likewise he who honours his mother is happy.
(Udanavarga, xxx, v. 23)

****

The succouring of mother and father, the cherishing of child and wife, and the following of a lawful calling, this is the greatest blessing.
(Mahamangala Sutta, v. 5)

****

Whoever, being able[to do so], does not support his feeble and aged mother or father, know him as a Vasala (slave).

Whoever strikes, or abuses by words, his mother, father, brother, sister, or mother-in-law, know him as a Vasala.

Research Recommended

Extensive knowledge and science, well-regulated discipline and well-spoken speech, this is the greatest blessing.

(Mahamangala Sutta, v. 4)

****

The world exists by cause; all things exist by cause; all beings are bound by cause, [even] as the rolling cart-wheel by the pin of an axletree.

(Vasettha Sutta, v. 61)

****

From whomsoever a man learns the Law, he should worship him, even as the gods worship Indra. The learned man, being thus honoured, his mind pleased with [his disciple], makes the Law more manifest.

(Nava Sutta, v. 1)

The Moral Law Inexorable

There exists no spot on the earth, or in the sky, or in the sea, neither is there any in the mountain-clefts, where an [evil deed does not bring trouble to the doer].*

(Udanavarga, ix, v. 5)

* A man can never escape punishment for evil Karma, nor can anyone deprive him of the reward of his good Karma. A Buddhist friend asks me to here recall the case of the robber, Angulimala, who, becoming converted by Lord Buddha, attained the state of Arhat. But this does not alter the principle here stated. Angulimala's Karma was to be, first a robber, and then a saint.

****

The evil doer suffers in this world, and he suffers in the next; he suffers in both. He suffers when he thinks of the evil he has done; he suffers more when going on the evil path. (Dhammapada, v. 17)

****

Surely an evil deed does not turn on a sudden like milk [curdling]; it is like fire smouldering in the ashes, which burns the fool. . . . . An evil deed kills not instantly, as does a sword, but it follows the evil doer [even] into the next world.

- (Udanavarga, ix, vv. 16, 17)

****

All that we are is the result of what we have thought: it is founded on our thoughts, it is made up of our thoughts. If a man speaks or acts with a pure thought, happiness follows him, like a shadow that never leaves him.

(Dhammapada, v. 2)

[16]

Adeptship a Fact

The Rahat* is able to fly through the air, change his appearance, fix the years of his life, shake heaven and earth.

(Sutra of the 42 Sections, Beal's Catena, p. 191)

* Adept or Mahatma.

****

Matanga, the Doctor of the Law, having before this arrived at the condition of a Rahat,forthwith, by his miraculous power, ascended up into space and there exhibited himself, undergoing various spiritual changes, e.g., flying, walking, sitting, sleeping and so on.

Hereupon was a rain of precious flowers, so that the feelings of the beholders were deeply moved, etc.

(Ming Ti pen niu chouen. Beal's trans.)

****

Lord Buddha's aunt, Mahaprajapati,and five other holy women, who lived according to the rules, "walked on the water as on dry land; others leaving the ground, walked in the air,or sat, or lay down, or stood still, all in the same element. Fire and water were seen flowing from the right side of some, and from the left side of others. In others it was seen issuing from their mouths." *

(Edkin's Chinese Buddhism, p. 49)

*Bishop Bigandet, in his Legend of Gaudama, and Rev. S. Beal, in his Catena of Buddhist Scriptures, give many data with respect to the powers (iddhi) attained by Rahats (Adepts, or "Mahatmas").

****

At a great assembly of the gods, Buddha, thinking that it would be better if his discourse was delivered to them in the form of a dialogue, and finding that the gods were backward to join in the dialogue, created a duplicate of himself,** who,standing before him put the questions which Gotama has answered in the Sammaparibbajaniya Sutta. (See translation by Sir Coomara Swamy.)

** Or, as expressed in modern scientific language, "projected his own double, or astral body." An aged priest in the Southern Province of Ceylon kindly gave me a small silver toy representing this phenomenon. It is called Samparana. (For an account of the wonders, see Bigandet's Legend of Gaudama, Vol. 1).

****

The True Buddhists Priest

There are four kinds of priests; not a fifth,O Chunda! Whoever has crossed all his doubts, is freed from the dart (of sorrow), attached to Nibbana, divested of greediness, the guide of all the world and the gods, such an one the Buddhas call Maggajina [the victorious wayfarer].

Whoever, knowing here the best as the best, preaches and discourses extensively on it; him [the Buddhas] declare to be the doubt-cutting sage, who is freed from desire, the second of priests,Maggadesi [who teaches the way]. Whoever lives in the paths which are taught [as] the Paths of the Law, well trained, possessed of a good memory, him they call the third priest, Maggajivi [who follows the blameless paths].

He who, putting on the garb of well-conducted men,*[yet rushes] forward [to acquire different objects], and brings disgrace on families, [and being] forward, hypocritical, ill trained,babbling, walks in the garden of good men, is a Maggadusi [who defiles the way].

(Chunda Sutta)

* The robes of the Buddhist monk.

****

Whoever,not being a sanctified person, pretends to be a saint, he indeed is the lowest Vasala,** the thief in all worlds, including that of Brahma.

(Vasala Sutta, v. 20)

** A slave.

****

A priest fond of quarreling - hemmed in by the attributes of ignorance, understands not the advice [given by others], nor the Law preached by Buddha;

Led away by ignorance, he knows not that quarreling is injurious to those whose hearts are practiced in religion, and that it is sinful, [and] a road to hell.

Such a priest, going to hell, flits [thence] from womb to womb,* from darkness to darkness, [and] certainly meets with affliction.

(Dhammachariya Sutta, vv. 3, 4, 5)

* In constant rebirths.

****

Of old there were only three diseases, [viz.],desire, want of food, decay. Owing to the killing of cattle there sprang ninety-eight diseases.

This old sin of injuring[living beings] has comedown [to this day]. Innocent cows are killed. Priests have fallen off from their virtues.

Thus this old [and] mean act is despised by the wise. Men despise a priest in whom such vice is found.

(Brahmanadhammika Sutta, vv. 29, 30, 31)

****

Some fortify themselves for controversy. We praise not those small-minded persons; temptations from here and there are made to cling to them and they certainly send their minds very far away when engaged in it.

(Dhammika Sutta, v. 15).

****

The priest who, like one who seeks flowers on fig-trees, has not found any more good in repeated births, gives up Orapara,* as a snake [casts off its] decayed old skin.

The priest in whose heart there are no feelings of anger [and] who likewise has gone past merit and demerit, gives up Orapara, etc.

(Uraga Sutta, vv. 5, 6)

*i.e., destroys that yearning for life in the body which results in rebirth.

****

Many men whose shoulders are covered with the orange robes are ill-conditioned and unrestrained; such evil-doers by their evil deeds go to hell.

(Dhammapada, v. 307)

****

He whose head is shaven, and who wears the saffron-coloured robe, but who seeks only for food, drink, clothes and bedding, is his [own] greatest enemy.

(Udanavarga, xiii, v. 14)

****

He who smites will be smitten; he who shows rancour will find rancour; so likewise from reviling, comes reviling and to him who is angered comes anger.

(Udanavarga, xiv, v. 3)

****

Those foolish priests who know not the holy law, though this life be brief, in the foolishness of their hearts they give themselves to wrangling.

(Udanavarga, xiv, vi 4)

****

"He abused me, he reviled me, he beat me, he subdued me"; who keeps this in his mind, and who feels resentment, will find no peace.

(Dhammapada, xiv, v. 4)

****

Like a beautiful flower full of colour but without scent, are the fine but fruitless words of him who does not act accordingly.

(Dhammapada, v. 51)

****

One is the road that heads to Wealth, another the road that leads to Nirvana.

(Dhammapada, v. 75)

****

If a man consorting with me [Buddha] does not conform his life to my commandments, what benefit will ten thousand precepts be to him?

(Sutra of the 42 Sections, Beal's Catena, p. 202)

****

Better it would be that a man should eat a hump of flaming iron than that one who is unrestrained and who has broken his vows should live on the charity of the land.

(Udanavarga, ix, v. 2)

****

If thou hast done evil deeds, if thou wouldst do them, thou mayest arise and run where'er thou wilt, but thou canst not free thyself of thy suffering.

(Udanavarga, ix, v. 4)

****

The thoughtless man even if he can recite Manygathas, but is not a doer of the law, has no part in the priesthood, but is like a cowherd counting the cows of others.

(Dhammapada, v. 19)

****

Who is the good man? The religious man only is good. Who is the great man? He who is strongest in the exercise of patience. He who patiently endures injury, and maintains a blameless life - he is a man indeed!

(Sutra of the 42 Sections, Beal's Catena, p. 196)

****

When a fire is placed under a pot, and the water within it made to boil, then whoever looks down upon it will see no shadow of himself. So the three poisons(covetousness, anger, delusion), and the five obscurities (envy,passion, sloth, vacillation, unbelief) which embrace it, effectually prevent one attaining supreme reason.

(Sutra of the 42 Sections, Beal's Catena, p. 196)

****

A man who is under the influence of religious principle may be compared to a single warrior opposed to ten thousand in a fight.

(Sutra of the 42 Sections, Beal's Catena, p. 200)

****

If one man conquer in battle a thousand times thousand men, and if another conquer himself, he is the greatest of conquerors.

(Dhammapada, v. 103)

****

By oneself evil is done, by oneself one suffers; by oneself evil is left undone, by oneself one is purified. Purity and impurity belong to oneself, no one can purify another.

(Dhammapada, v. 165)

****

Self is the lord of self; who else could be the lord? With self well subdued, a man finds a master such as few can find.

(Dhammapada, v. 160)

****

That priest whose[ideas of] omens, meteors, dreams and signs are destroyed, and who is released from[a belief in] the evil consequences of omens, conducts himself well in the world. That priest who, not quarreling in word, thought or deed,[and]knowing the Law well looks forward to Nirvana, conducts himself well in the world.

(Sammaparibbajaniya Sutta, vv. 2. 7)

****

Kinsfolk, friends and lovers salute a man who has been long away, and returns from afar. In like manner his good works receive him who has done good, and has gone from this world to the other; as kinsmen receive a friend on his return.

(Dhammapada, vv. 219, 220)

****

Even a good man sees evil days, as long as his good deed is not ripened: but when his good deed has ripened, then does the good man see happy days.

(Dhammapada, v. 120)

****

In fit time, observe kindness, impartiality, mercy, freedom from sin, delight at the prosperity of others; unopposed to the whole world, let one walk alone like the rhinoceros.

(Khaggavisana Sutta, 39)

****

If a man's thoughts are not dissipated, if his mind is not perplexed, if he has ceased to think of good and evil, then there is no fear for him while he is watchful.

(Dhammapada, v. 39)

****

Procrastination is[moral] defilement, continued procrastination is defilement. By non procrastination [punctuality] and knowledge, root out your darts [of sin].

(Utthana Sutta, v. 4)

First printed as a Pamphlet in 1887

Certificate

MALIGAKANDA,

November 27, 1887

I HAVE read Colonel Wolcott's compilation of moral precepts from the Buddhist Scriptures, and recommend the same as a book of instruction for Buddhist youth.

- H. Sumangala,

High Priest.

THE END

THE END

Made in the USA
Middletown, DE
16 June 2019